FROM THE MIND OF CRITIC

2016

BY: BRYAN RADZIN

FROM THE MIND OF CRITIC

2016

©2017 LULU, ALL RIGHTS RESERVED

ISBN# 978-0-578-19448-6

UNRELENTING POSITIVITY

AUTHOR: BRYAN RADZIN

COVER PHOTOS: BRYAN RADZIN

I DEDICATE THIS TO ANYBODY WHO HAS EVER BEEN LOST IN A SEA OF CHAOS AND CONFUSION. WE FIND OUR TRUE NORTH, WHEN WE REALIZE IT HAS BEEN WITHIN US THE WHOLE TIME.

ACKNOWLEDGEMENTS

Thank you Mom for your non-stop support and love, it's the exact motivation I need in sharing my love and support to help the world consciously evolve. Thank you Dad for proving that when I set my mind to something, I really can make it happen. Thank you Lisa for bringing me back down to earth, when I'm floating in the clouds. Thank you Melody for fully understanding the creative spirit that flows through our veins, we will positively change the world. Thank you Sean for the bursts of consciousness, it's historically perceptive people like you that poke through propaganda like a hot knife through butter. Thank you Tim for being one of the few people I know who truly "gets" that we fix dishonesty in government, by fixing dishonesty within ourselves. Thank you Laurie for opening my mind to the consciousness that the universe has to offer, I am a better human being because of our conversations.

PROLOGUE

Is there ever a time when something so crazy happens, that we throw up our hands and say screw it? Has the darkest part of our soul ever taken control over our critical thinking skills, and destroyed the good nature that we were brought up on? Have we been hiding our true thoughts and feelings for so long, than when society needs us to express the full breadth of our goodness, we clam up because we're afraid of what other people might say? Whether it was Nixon, Reagan, Bush or Trump, we have been confronted with the animalistic side of our emotions time and time again. In this the 17th year of our new millennium, let's try something different. Better put, let's try something that we've been afraid of ever since loud voices started shouting down reasonable points of view. We all need to take humanity, accountability, love, peace, justice, understanding and critical thought, and share it with people we disagree with. The conversations that spawn will prove that the only thing keeping us from uniting, is ourselves. Compromise isn't a dirty word, and becomes more beautiful when we realize our fear of it, is what has been holding us back. ☺

FROM THE MIND OF CRITIC

JANUARY 1st 2016

From the mind of critic: "Is the new year that's now upon us a clean slate, a new beginning, a blank canvas or an empty drawing board? Is this day different from every other day because we're required to start fresh? Do we just think this day is different, when in actuality we can start fresh at any moment of any day? There's an old saying that goes "fool me once shame on you, fool me twice shame on me". We need to stop fooling ourselves into thinking that we have no say in what happens to us. If so many other people are stronger, faster, smarter, richer, luckier or better looking than us, how could we possibly succeed in our passions? We can un-fool ourselves by creating a new beginning anytime the mood strikes. We don't have to wait until a man-made time change happens, we can surprise ourselves by evolving anytime we choose." ☺

FROM THE MIND OF CRITIC

JANUARY 2nd 2016

From the mind of critic: "If the scales of justice are lopsided one way or another, does either side receive justice? If a rich person gets away with running somebody over and killing them while drunk, and a poor person gets convicted of manslaughter, does either receive justice? If a police officer gets away with shooting somebody of one race because they were scared, but goes to prison for shooting somebody of another race, even though the circumstances were exactly the same, does either receive justice? We have major race and class issues that have been around since the beginning of time. With that said, if we ever hope to get past them, criminal penalties must be the same no matter the color of somebody's skin, or how much money is in their bank account. Accountability through humanism is how we level the playing field, and clear the road blocks that prevent us from evolving. None of us have justice, until we all have justice. None of us are accountable, until we're all accountable." ☺

FROM THE MIND OF CRITIC

JANUARY 5th 2016

From the mind of critic: "If we're told that our guns are being taken away, but no evidence exists beyond anecdotes, where does that leave us? If we're told that we're being overrun by radical Muslim terrorists, when statistics show more people are killed by radical Christian terrorists, where does that leave us? If we're told that so many people are flooding over the Mexican border that we need to build a wall, when statistics show most illegal immigration takes place by people from Europe and Asia overstaying their visas, where does that leave us? You know where I'm going with this. We're told a lot of crazy shit about the threats we face, most of the time to push an agenda. We must realize that fear and racism clouds our critical thinking, causing us to blindly follow whoever yells the loudest. Our biggest threat isn't guns, terrorists or immigrants, it's us not asking critical questions." ☺

FROM THE MIND OF CRITIC

JANUARY 6th 2016

From the mind of critic: "If we go down the rabbit hole whether willingly or unwillingly, will we believe what we witness? Will we take what we see, and use it for our own betterment, even if it changes the inherent meaning? Will we try to hold the information over people to prove we're smarter, which down to the letter proves why we're not smarter? With the media tsunami 24-7 365, it's hard to know where the rabbit hole is, or who it belongs to. We decipher what's constructive to our evolution, and what's not by paying attention. When we're given indisputable statistics, we shouldn't say what we think they mean. We should take them in, and then do something about the problems they address. Statistics for violent crimes can be skewed by changing definitions, but when there's mass shooting after mass shooting; the only thing that's skewed is our minds when we think we can't do anything. If guns aren't the problem but people are, we should just fix people, and stop endlessly talking about it. If we think we can't solve a problem, is it because we aren't allowing ourselves to find a solution? ☺

FROM THE MIND OF CRITIC

JANUARY 7th 2016

From the mind of critic: "If all clouds have a silver lining, do massacres and terrorist attacks have a good side? Is there really a positive and negative to all events? Is it just something we say to make ourselves feel better? When people ask hypotheticals, they tend to use extreme examples. This is so the mind is forced to make a decision. All of life does come down to choices, but none of us know what we'd do in a crazy situation unless it was presently happening. It's impossible to ponder an on the fly decision in advance, or it wouldn't on the fly. Life is balanced into positive and negative camps. We must figure out which one we're in now, not later." ☺

FROM THE MIND OF CRITIC
JANUARY 8th 2016

From the mind of critic: "If somebody said they were going to take your guns away, that would freak you out right? If somebody said they weren't going to take your guns away, that would make you feel better right? If the person accused of taking guns away is simply attempting to check if somebody has a violent history, before allowing them to buy a gun, should it freak anybody out? There's so much hypocrisy in this country, it's maddening sometimes. When ideas are peddled, that a law abiding citizen has a harder time buying a gun, because they have to prove they're the law abiding citizen they say they are, it's no wonder people think their guns are being taken away. People can hear something over and over, that it causes them to actually believe that since criminals will always break the law, that we shouldn't have laws for anything. If you want anarchy fine, just come right out and say it, don't portray yourself as a patriotic American. Honesty is the only policy that will move us forward." ☺

FROM THE MIND OF CRITIC

JANUARY 9th 2016

From the mind of critic: "If the United States Constitution guarantees a trial by a jury of our peers, where does that leave us when our peers do whatever they can to get out of jury duty? If we say we should help out our fellow humans when they need it, but then do whatever we can to escape when the opportunity presents itself, where does that leave us? Is all our conscious and evolutionary talk a bunch of hot air, covering up the fact that we don't give a shit about anybody but ourselves? A lot of us out there don't care, but a lot of us do. We care about the environment, justice, fairness, equality, diversity, humanity and accountability. Some of us just haven't moved from words into actions. Until we do, our dreams won't come true. Knowing how to help our fellow man and actually doing it, are two different things. When we figure that out, nothing will stop us." ☺

FROM THE MIND OF CRITIC

JANUARY 12th 2016

From the mind of critic: "If self-hate turns into jealousy, does jealousy turn into hate of others? If hate of others turns into forming a group based on that hate, does that group use religion to justify its actions? Does using a religious doctrine to justify a hate group's actions, prove that every religion has its fundamentalists? No religion is free from crazies, and no religion has more than the other. If somebody says one religion breeds crazy while another simply maintains it, that person is feeding into the false narrative that creates fundamentalists in the first place. How do we stop fundamentalists from screaming so loud that we can't hear our own critical thinking skills? We stop hating ourselves. How do we do that? We focus on what we love and what we have, instead of what we hate and what we don't have. If nobody is free from self-hate, nobody is free from fundamentalism. To be who we really are, we have to see people for who they really are." ☺

FROM THE MIND OF CRITIC

JANUARY 13th 2016

From the mind of critic: "If we really want the next generation to be better than ours, are we setting them up for success by cutting regulations, so the free market can flow completely unfettered? Are we setting them up for failure by only allowing the biggest, loudest, richest and most influential voices to be heard? Do we think the next generation is screwed anyway, so why even think about it? Many Native American tribes and cultures look seven generations down the line when making major decisions, why not Americans? Are we scared? Excited? Jealous? Maybe a gene is embedded in our DNA, that forces us to screw over our fellow human beings on our road to success. Low self-esteem causes us to want total control over our environment, labor, military, health care, finances and politics. When we step outside of our box, we'll see that making things good for those who come after us, makes life better now, because it teaches us what's really important. All generations are an extension of this moment right now. Accountability people, come on." ☺

FROM THE MIND OF CRITIC
JANUARY 14th 2016

From the mind of critic: "If we feel control slipping away, do we overcompensate by trying to control every detail? Do we give up trying to control anything, and float through life by way of whichever way the wind blows? Do we balance control and compromise so we don't alienate those close to us? Feeling like we don't have control over anything, makes us just as crazy as feeling like we have to control everything. We find balance in the middle by realizing we can control somethings, our eating, words, reactions, deeds, actions and thoughts. We can't control what people think, feel, act or say. Having the courage to know what we can and can't control, comes through the trial and error scavenger hunt we call life. We must never fall into the trap of ridiculing and criticizing what we don't think is good enough. Chances are we're projecting to the letter what's wrong with us. Accountability to self is only control we really need." ☺

FROM THE MIND OF CRITIC

JANUARY 15th 2016

From the mind of critic: "If the most dangerously violent tool of all mankind is a pen, why all the saber rattling with guns, bombs and indiscriminate black ops? Why threaten a country with carpet bombing, when a much more dangerous weapon comes in a ten pack for $2? Is the ignorance and self-importance these violence purveyors peddle, nothing more than a cover for how powerful a pen really is? We've all heard that the pen is mightier than the sword, which you'd think would make more people use one. You'd think more people would use their words to articulate a problem, before articulating a solution. Some of us are lazy when we pick up a gun instead of a pen to make the changes we seek. We might think beating our enemies into oblivion is easier than using our words. Is murder really easier than talking? We'll never succeed in life if we always take the easy way out. Great change requires great effort." ☺

FROM THE MIND OF CRITIC

JANUARY 16th 2016

From the mind of critic: "If the sword gets its power from the pen, what gives the pen its power? Are thoughts and feelings the ink that's in the pen, guiding it towards using the sword as the only viable solution? If the pen is mightier than the sword, are thoughts mightier than the pen? Thoughts and feelings drive our words, and words drive our actions. We have to get our thoughts moving in the right direction, which can be difficult depending on our environment and life experience. We can break the cycle of racism, sexism and classism by seeing ourselves as we really are, and then seeing others how they really are. This makes us realize how we want to be treated. Basically it all boils down to the golden rule. Thoughts can be ruthless, but if we see each other in ourselves, the thoughts that go into the pen which influences the sword will be of construction, not destruction. The pen has always been powerful, but becomes infinitely more so when our true soul is bared." ☺

FROM THE MIND OF CRITIC

JANUARY 19th 2016

From the mind of critic: "If we must build up positive energy to go after our passion, what happens after we expend that energy working our passion? What happens when our energy is zapped? Do we go after what makes us happy in the short run, and fill ourselves up with a small amount of energy that's detrimental in the long run? Does it reveal issues that have been covered up by us working our passion? Burying ourselves in work so we don't obsess about situations or issues is a healthy thing. It becomes unhealthy when we've buried ourselves so much, that when we take a short break from that work, our issues flood back ten times stronger because we've ignored them. How do we avoid using our passion as an escape? How do we make sure our issues don't fog over our passion? We search for balance. We make sure we don't live to feed our passion, we make sure we feed our passion to live." ☺

FROM THE MIND OF CRITIC

JANUARY 20th 2016

From the mind of critic: "When we're honest with ourselves about who we are, is it easier to spot others who are honest with themselves about who they are? Do lies and fakeness breed lies and fakeness, just like honesty and authenticity breed honesty and authenticity? Do we bring the energy we possess, or just the energy we portray? Being honest with ourselves when we're happy, excited, motivated and determined is easy. It's a lot harder when we're sad, afraid, lonely and can't see the future. We must realize being honest with ourselves in the bad times, makes the good times brighter. This isn't because we're reveling in our own misery, making it plummet to previously unknown depths. It's because when we celebrate the good times while escaping the bad, the bad will hit 10 times harder, and we'll have turned ourselves bipolar. If honesty is the best policy, then making it through the bad times, will make us feel like we've earned the good times. All of us deserve the good times, will we do the work required?" ☺

FROM THE MIND OF CRITIC

JANUARY 21st 2016

From the mind of critic: "If life isn't a drag race, why do we speed through it at 330 MPH? If life is short, why don't we speed through it at 330? If our time is limited, how do we slow down and enjoy life, while still accomplishing as much as we possibly can? Finding balance in our free time, work time, friend time, play life, love life and dream life is difficult, and will never be perfect. That doesn't mean we stop trying, and that doesn't mean we'll never succeed. It just means that nothing in life is guaranteed, whether we speed through life or we crawl. We just need to figure out how to spend time, and not waste time, while we enjoy time. How do we do that? We realize time is a man-made construct, and can be as long or short as we want it to be. Depending on what occupies our minds, will determine how long or short time seems. It isn't about speeding or slowing through life, it's about enjoying our journey and uplifting our soul, specifically so we can uplift others." ☺

FROM THE MIND OF CRITIC

JANUARY 22nd 2016

From the mind of critic: "If a smiling blue sky is all we see, are we ignoring everything else? If positive thoughts of the beauty surrounding us are the first thing on our mind, are we deleting all others? Are we changing our perception so as to not blind ourselves, but to truly see life and what's important? Some of us get blinded by the light when we only see what's positive and bright, because it gives us the false impression that it's the only thing that exists. When something bad does happen, it might cause us to go into crisis mode because we don't know how to handle it. Some of us choose positivity, realizing it's not sunshine and roses all the time. When we breathe beauty into our soul, it carries us through the bad times, which become shorter and leave a smaller footprint. How we perceive life is how we live it. We just have to ask ourselves what produces the best results." ☺

FROM THE MIND OF CRITIC

JANUARY 23th 2016

From the mind of critic: "If we don't know how to handle a crisis, do we flip out because we're bombarded by all the ways we can't fix the situation? Do we hunker down and hunt for solutions? Do we ask critical questions of ourselves and our perception, so we know if it's actually a crisis? We can build a lot up in our head that make things sound worse than they actually are. Sometimes we're scared, nervous and confused that answers don't immediately appear. We might even hope, wish and pray for a better day, because we think no action can change anything, or it would have happened already. We need to realize that a crisis whether real or imaginary, only has power over us if we let it. Reclaiming power consists of determining if a crisis is for personal, political or religious gain. Once we determine its category, we'll find the right tools to fix it. If our perceptions define what we see, are crises' always in our head? Are they always figments of our imagination?" ☺

FROM THE MIND OF CRITIC

JANUARY 26th 2016

From the mind of critic: "If somebody has New York values as opposed to Texas values, as opposed to California values as opposed to Oklahoma, Mississippi or Montana values, do any of the people that live there actually represent those values? Does pretentious and false labeling help our feeble minds make sense out of a chaotic world? Does it inhibit us, so we can only achieve our goals through lies, judgment and false promises? Any of us can say anybody is a certain way to prove a point, just like polls can be funded to prove a point, just like paid experts can testify in jury trials to prove a point. Knowing all that, we must be vigilantly skeptical of anybody trying to persuade us to do something they want, because tall tales only hold up on the surface. How do we take away their power? If we critically think and ask questions, phony prophets and false idols won't know what hit them." ☺

FROM THE MIND OF CRITIC

JANUARY 27th 2016

From the mind of critic: "if we do what we can when we feel there is nothing we can do, what do we do when we can't think anymore? When we get bombarded by our jobs, families and our daily routine, what happens when we're asked about the million other things going on in the world? Does our mind spin, causing it to curl up in the philosophical fetal position? Does our mind surprise us by reorganizing, rearranging and reprioritizing so we can achieve what we didn't think possible? Being emotionally and spiritually exhausted, takes just as much out of us as being physically exhausted. When we combine all 3 it creates the perfect storm, testing the deepest part of our soul created character. Once we realize that we do for ourselves specifically so we can do for others, we'll see anything outside our circle will flow freely because we're not preoccupied. A mind is a terrible thing to waste, let's not waste ours and become incomplete human beings" ☺

FROM THE MIND OF CRITIC

JANUARY 28th 2016

From the mind of critic: "If we spend all our time worrying about the next big thing, or the next big hurdle, when do we have time to plan? If all we do is worry about what we don't have and haven't done, when do we lay the foundation for accomplishments? Does worrying accomplish anything, or does it distract us from taking action because we've analyzed too much? I don't know where the old saying "don't be a worry wart" came from, but if we hope to accomplish what we need to do to survive, let alone what hugs our soul, we can't be a worry wart. We can't only focus on the negative, and automatically switch off our brains to anything that takes effort. We must focus on a balance of the positive and the negative, so we know how bad and good life can get, and won't obsess about either. Once we realize that we only move forward when we plan for the future by not ignoring it, we'll witness worry disappear from our thought process." ☺

FROM THE MIND OF CRITIC

JANUARY 29th 2016

From the mind of critic: "If we truly want to make the changes that will move us as a species forward, will we get to the root of problems? Will we refrain from changing our placeholders once again this election season? Why do we need political parties at all? Why do we need the Electoral College? Why can't we gauge the winner by the popular vote? If we don't want government to control our lives, why do we insist on laws that do just that? Why do we get surprised if the government doesn't work right and is the problem, when we keep electing people who prove it? Does handing decision making abilities over to the richest among us, ever produce an office holder who truly fights for the people? There are so many more questions we could ask. It would take an entire book to list them all. We must keep asking, and then we must act. Are we ready to take the next step?" ☺

FROM THE MIND OF CRITIC

JANUARY 30th 2016

From the mind of critic: "If the moral arc of the universe is long but bends toward justice, how long is the arc? Are we supposed to wait for justice, because the moral arc is aimed there? Does fighting for what we believe in cause the moral arc to shorten? In the history of human evolution, we've been through many terrible events. It eventually ends, then we learn lessons and things get a little better, pretty much Darwin's definition of evolution. What we're continuing to learn, is that we control the speed of our evolution. Outside forces can guide us in a certain direction, by stating reasons how and why we should evolve. It's us who can say hey, I'm standing up and making change because it's the right thing to do, starting with myself. When enough of us realize this, the moral arc will bend to our will because we'll be evolving into a better world." ☺

FROM THE MIND OF CRITIC

FEBRUARY 2nd 2016

From the mind of critic: "If we plan so much that we know something inside and out, do we half-ass the work because it feels like we've already worked hard enough? Is it a cop out to put all our energy into strategizing, instead of action because our strategy feels like action? Are we scared of acting, so we plan until we get tired and then move on? Do we know life is 90% prep work to make sure it's focused and meaningful? Having thoughts, ideas, dreams and goals keep us headed in the right direction, because we're picturing a better future. Problems occur when we fail to bring those thoughts from inside our head, to in front of our face. Once we realize our mind moves us forward when it shows us the work that needs to be done, not the work that is being done, we'll see we really do control our destiny. Planning is never a bad thing. We just have to find planning that works for us, so we can act in a way which benefits us." ☺

FROM THE MIND OF CRITIC
FEBRUARY 3rd 2016

From the mind of critic: "If we truly want to rock the Kasbah, do we carpet bomb them into oblivion so they are truly rocked through and through? Do we inundate them with American propaganda through news and music, so they become more American like us, and less scary like them? Do we show them a universal language they can relate to, because it touches our human core? If anybody hasn't seen the original music video to the Clash's "Rock the Kasbah", you should YouTube it right now. The image of a Bedouin Arab and an Orthodox Jew coming together, and rocking out to good music they both could relate to, is a lesson for all human kind. Music, along with food can break down barriers, and allow us to experience cultures in an authentic way, not a falsely intellectual one. Seeing each other in ourselves is how we evolve. Once we realize this, not only will we rock the Kasbah, we will rock the world." ☺

FROM THE MIND OF CRITIC

FEBRUARY 4th 2016

From the mind of critic: "Is allowing more pollution through the clear skies initiative, like saying you're a progressive who wants to keep things the way they are? Is saying one thing and doing another just how politics are played, or is it a symptom of how life is played? Do politicians lie to us because they are us, and we lie to each other? Whether we portray ourselves differently from how we act, or portray a false image so we don't have to act, we have many instances when we're dishonest with ourselves. We might think we aren't good enough to show people who we really are, and say what we really mean, but we are. Even if we're scared of the reactions we'll get when we peer from behind our rock, we can't be scared. Once we realize that we can't hide or pull one over on people by portraying ourselves falsely, we'll see our confidence level rise, and our soul grow. Not being rude makes the world a friendly place, not being truthful takes away our chance to evolve." ☺

FROM THE MIND OF CRITIC

FEBRUARY 5th 2016

From the mind of critic: "If there's more cops in poor neighborhoods than rich ones, is it an indication of who the bigger criminal is, or who commits a higher volume of crime? Is it simply a case of a population with the resources and influence to get away with more crime? We never seem to bat an eye if some clean cut person strolls down the street in an expensive suit, but damn if we don't get all up in arms if we see a dirty, ragged and stinky homeless person cavorting down the street. Sometimes we're afraid of what's different, and feel safe around what appears to be the same. Once we realize the inner debate of, do rich people commit more crime because they can get away with more, or commit less crime because of no financial concerns, we'll see that poor people commit the same amount of crime, they just get harassed more. Cops might patrol more in poor neighborhoods than rich ones, but that's only because cops support the rich by keeping all the poor people in line. If money is the root of all evil, cops are the fertilizer that makes those roots strong." ☺

FROM THE MIND OF CRITIC

FEBRUARY 6th 2016

From the mind of critic: "When light is so dim that we can't see what's out there, but can hear it, do we run and hide? Do we excitedly listen harder so we can determine what's out there, even if it hasn't come into view? Is there a third way, where we aren't scared or excited, but open? When thousands of geese fly over my head before it gets totally dark, I can't see them, but man, can I hear them, and they're loud. It's much the same when we move forward. We realize there's some noise and distraction we can see, but most we can't. We know it's out there, but it doesn't have an image because we haven't associated one with it. Do we picture heavenly geese migrating, or do we picture an angry mob squelching positive change? If life is all about perception, then what we perceive is true, becomes true. Life is more than a positive and negative balance, it's a revolving door of possibilities. Will we walk through?" ☺

FROM THE MIND OF CRITIC
FEBRUARY 9th 2016

From the mind of critic: "If moving forward with blinders on eliminates distractions, does it also eliminate the joy and beauty of the world because all we see is our journey forward? If the endpoint is all we see, will we step on anybody or anything to get there? Once we get to the endpoint, what do we see? Do we keep chasing the dragon because endpoints are an illusion? Being focused on our goals and dreams is never a bad thing, but we must always remember there's no such thing as an endpoint. We will never arrive at a place where everything is perfect, and no work has to be done. Once we realize that it's detrimental to strive toward an endpoint, but extremely motivational to move in the right direction, we'll find not only our purpose in life, but also the joy that has proven elusive. Focusing on what's important to all of us, keeps us moving in the right direction. Focusing on what's important only to us, cements our blinders. We just have to figure out what's more beneficial to the planet" ☺

FROM THE MIND OF CRITIC

FEBRUARY 10th 2016

From the mind of critic: "Does washing away, praying away, absolving or moving past sins make them disappear, because somebody in a position of authority said they would? Do we expect all the bad stuff we've ever done to be forgiven by somebody waving a philosophical magic wand? Does this give us free reign to do whatever we want regardless of the consequences? Blind faith in anything is just that, blinding. If we are so lazy that we look for any excuse to not ask the tough questions, there will always be a small group of people controlling our thoughts. Life is hard I'm not denying that, but we must never forget that good, great and beautiful things are achievable if we put in the effort. If we accept responsibility for our actions, we become accountable to ourselves. Once we become accountable, we gain control of our own lives. Once we have control, we won't need blind faith or absolution, because we'll have dealt with our own shit, ourselves. Won't that save the world?" ☺

FROM THE MIND OF CRITIC

FEBRUARY 11th 2016

From the mind of critic: "Does the pink, orange and purple awesomeness of a sunrise always wash away the preceding darkness? Does an old day always get pushed out by a new dawn? Do we just say tomorrow will be different because we can't see any feasible way to make today any better? The sooner we realize that today, this moment, now is the first day of the rest of our lives, the sooner we'll realize we can live our life authentically anytime we want. Whether it's darkness, light or something in-between, there are lessons we can learn if we're open to them. Balance is important. If we're awash in darkness, we could get blinded by light because we don't know how to deal. On the same token, if we're awash in light, we don't want to get blinded by the darkness because we don't know how to deal. Sunrise, sunsets and all earth's natural beauty will always beat out the darkness, but only if we choose to see it that way." ☺

FROM THE MIND OF CRITIC

FEBRUARY 12th 2016

From the mind of critic: "if every action causes a reaction, does every reaction compensate for inaction? Do some reactions come from not acting personally, while others simply happen because we're human? Are actions and reactions the same because they both require action, and arguing their difference is like arguing whether the chicken or the egg came first? I think we could all agree that doing something because it's the right thing to do, and waiting for somebody else to do something while we play Monday morning quarterback, are two totally different concepts. We get caught up when we concentrate on the labels and words we use, instead of concentrating on just doing the right thing. I hate to say that our positive and collective evolution depends on us not talking the talk but walking the walk, but if the shoe fits..........." ☺

FROM THE MIND OF CRITIC

FEBRUARY 13th 2016

From the mind of critic: "If nothing lasts forever, how come we hang on to what doesn't serve us? Do we cling to what causes our downfall because it's comfortable? Does it take away any need to change? If we know good things don't last forever, why don't we enjoy them while they're here, so we're ready and willing to accept new good times when they happen? Life is a constant ebb and flow of good times and bad times. We all get down on ourselves if things don't go our way, or feel like we're not good enough. Once we realize this feeling is temporary and can be replaced by positive thoughts and actions, we'll see we never have to cling to anything. We just have to see it, recognize it for what it is, and let it go. We find joy by choosing to see." ☺

FROM THE MIND OF CRITIC
FEBRUARY 16th 2016

From the mind of critic: "If we don't have the courage to say what we mean, and skulk around instead, is the corresponding energy drop like a 2x4 smacking us in the head, reminding us what happens when we stay quiet? Does this sneaking around fool anybody, or are we fooling ourselves when we think we can get what we want without effort? Once we realize all this, how do we pull ourselves back? Maybe we're lonely, have low self-esteem and can't specifically picture what we know in our heart we want. We might cut corners and take shortcuts because we're scared of the direct route. When we realize that what we want, need and dream requires an A to B line, not a zig zag switchback, we'll see that to make our dreams real, we must have courage. If we don't stand up for ourselves, who will? We can't wait for life to happen, we must make life happen with authentically concrete steps." ☺

FROM THE MIND OF CRITIC
FEBRUARY 17th 2016

From the mind of critic: "If we have to control every aspect of our lives, is it because we're out of control? Are we quick to point out deficiencies in others, specifically because we have those same deficiencies? Is this all meant to lessen the pain we feel, by making others feel worse? Many people bring us down during our daily routine, attempting to make us feel less than. Likewise, we do the same to others we interact with. Once we realize that if we dealt with our own issues, instead of pawning them off on others, we'll see that we critique others way less often, because we're critiquing ourselves. We project, and politicians project because we're the same. We fix the world by coming up with solutions for ourselves, not problems for others." ☺

FROM THE MIND OF CRITIC

FEBRUARY 18th 2016

From the mind of critic: "Do sinister motives guide all our actions whether conscious or subconscious, or does that only happen to politicians? Do people running for office rarely say what they mean, because we rarely say what we mean? If truth overpowers lies, does authenticity overpower people who portray themselves as something they're not? Regardless of our background, upbringing or environment, we all deserve to be heard, but only if we speak truthfully and utter we really think. Sometimes we're afraid somebody will become disagreeably violent if we express our feelings about an issue. We end up sugar coating everything, causing it to become what we think is more palatable. Once we realize disagreeing not only makes conversations more exciting but is also the foundation of our democracy, we'll see that having fiery conversations makes this country great, and using them to make it even better, keeps us evolving. Authenticity will save the world if we utilize authenticity." ☺

FROM THE MIND OF CRITIC
FEBRUARY 19th 2016

From the mind of critic: "Does voting matter when popular vote doesn't determine the winner? Does voting matter when unfettered Super PACs buy elections? Does one vote matter amongst 100 million? This is more than not being able to complain if we don't vote, everybody has a right to complain about government wrongs, whether we vote of not. Problems arise when we think that complaining is good enough. We think telling others about a problem will fix it, because they'll act in our place. It comes down to talking and acting. We must critically think, talk about what we want to do, and then do it. We must ask ourselves what we hope to accomplish by not voting. Do we want to bring down a corrupt system by not participating, specifically so we can build a new one in its place? If we vote we must ask, can the system be changed so it's accountable to the people, and not just its patrons? This is a multi-pronged attack with many angles and facets. The fact we can have this conversation without getting arrested, is what makes America great. Our creed will help us live out our collective meaning, like never before." ☺

FROM THE MIND OF CRITIC

FEBRUARY 20th 2016

From the mind of critic: "If this is the time of the season for loving, is it also the time of the season for peace, justice, equality, ending hate and spawning consciousness? Is time what we make of it, or are we what makes time? We all know life comes down to choices we make and reactions we have. Do we realize time is an illusion, and we have as much or as little as we think? When we put our faith in something, it becomes our reality. We can be an optimist, pessimist, good, bad, positive, negative and/or view life through infinite lenses, but we control our destiny and actions. Nobody can stop us from creating a better world. Nobody can stop our conscious and evolutionary journey except ourselves. If we yearn to make collective and positive change, and we answer yes, we must have faith we can succeed. We make our goals and dreams come true, by believing we can." ☺

FROM THE MIND OF CRITIC

FEBRUARY 23rd 2016

From the mind of critic: If nobody will break our stride whether they get off our cloud or not, do they slow us down? Do we know we have to keep moving, to defend against slowing down? If we move forward because the world moves forward, do we achieve a balance that'll sustain us throughout our journey? We all have thoughts, hopes and dreams, ideas we'd love to see in reality not solely in our imaginations. When we share with friends, family and others to make our dreams real by putting words to them, we get motivated to achieve. Our circle could also break our stride, by motivating us to go in the opposite direction. People will block, slow and stop us from achieving what we know in our soul is the right thing. If we want to evolve, nobody better break our stride." ☺

FROM THE MIND OF CRITIC

FEBRUARY 24th 2016

From the mind of critic: "If the revolution won't be televised, is it because the network execs haven't figured out how to profit? Is it not televised because it'll be on the radio, internet, magazines, newspapers, social media and/or word of mouth? Will the revolution not be televised because there is no such thing as the revolution, only the next one? There are signs in the mass media from time to time that reveal critical and free thinkers, anti-establishment voices and events that are enemies to the corporate media structure. Sometimes these signs are token responses to make the people think change is possible. Sometimes they're people that fought and clawed for representation. Once we realize TV has a strong voice against the status quo, we'll see the quicker these progressive voices become the norm and not another bread and circus act, the quicker the status quo will actually represent everybody. Revolutions and direct actions bring conscious change when we realize we control the status quo." ☺

FROM THE MIND OF CRITIC

FEBRUARY 25th 2016

From the mind of critic: "If a foundation is the most important part of a house, what about the materials in that foundation? If we use weak ingredients, will our structure be weak? If we use strong ingredients, will our structure be strong? Is it the same for life when we start our journey? We all know that starting off with a good base, is imperative if we want our structure to last. If we don't care if our structure crumbles, it doesn't matter if we have a foundation at all. Basically, it comes down to benefits in the short run, or the long run. Do we care what happens to only us right now, or what happens to all of us from now until 100 years from now? Once we see our choice is between fleeting happiness and long term joy, we realize prep work isn't so cumbersome. Building a strong foundation cultivates our motivation to succeed, and that's what we want to do, right?" ☺

FROM THE MIND OF CRITIC
FEBRUARY 26th 2016

From the mind of critic: "If a picture freezes a moment in time, is it an accurate portrayal of life as a whole? Is the breadth of our journey an amalgamation of all the moments we've experienced? Are all of us hurtling through space simply trying to muddle through the chaos, to find crumbs of happiness wherever we can? So many thousand, million, billion things are happening every day to our exponentially increasing population. It's hard to know what's real. Sometimes we take photos, so our mind can easily travel back to that special moment. Sometimes we hold onto these moments as examples of the best thing ever. This is when we sell ourselves short by not experiencing bigger and better things. Remembering that happy times make life worth living, keeps joy flowing through us. We must never obsess that a memory won't happen again, or it definitely will not." ☺

FROM THE MIND OF CRITIC

FEBRUARY 27th 2016

From the mind of critic: "If there's no place like home, how come those without a home get crapped on when they try to make one? If home is where we feel comfortable, safe and stable enough to better ourselves, how can we expect others to go out and better themselves when they don't have that stable jumping off point? If there by the grace of God go we, do the rest of us realize we could homeless at any moment? I'm not advocating to feel bad about what we have, quite the contrary. I'm advocating that we feel grateful for what we have, because many people have way less. Once we feel grateful for what we have, instead of anger over not attaining some fictional, focus grouped, and lab created vison of success, we'll see that having less isn't a measure of character, how we react to it is. We all need a home, we all need to feel safe and we all need to be loved. Once this is ingrained in our everyday thinking, we positively evolve as a people." ☺

FROM THE MIND OF CRITIC
MARCH 1st 2016

From the mind of critic: "If a voting public is stuck in the land of polar opposites, doesn't it make sense that their political candidates are as well? If there's no middle ground besides a group clinging to both sides at the same time, is it possible for that group to authentically tell the truth if they're having their cake and eating it too? Doesn't the huge shit show they call election season prove once again that we don't need political parties, but a political revolution? You might be able to tell who I support by my previous statement, but that's beside the point. Candidates trying to be Republican light or Democratic light, end up being something in the middle that nobody wants. People might not want extremes, but what they want even less is an imposter. We need to get rid of political parties. We need to get rid of extremes. Before we do that however, we have to be honest with where we're at. Once were honest about our polarization by making it Sanders vs Trump, then we can delve deeper. Before we get rid of an issue, we must recognize its contents." ☺

FROM THE MIND OF CRITIC
MARCH 2nd 2016

From the mind of critic: "If we start our day with low energy and a short fuse, does our fuse become longer if our day starts with high energy? Would we be more able to deal with assholes and whiny babies if our energy was positive? Would the littlest thing set us off, making the insignificant significant because negative energy coursed through our veins? There are always going to be jerks, whiners and egomaniacs who think they do everything right. They will purposely screw things up just to point out other's faults. We must work to break that cycle by not feeding into it, and inserting our positive energy. It can seem impossible when we're lonely, feel like nobody besides our families love us, and can't be honest with anybody. Gaining confidence and self-esteem can be extremely hard, but is worth it when our fuse gets longer. It's not that we put up with more shit when we feel good about ourselves, we just don't let shit get us down." ☺

FROM THE MIND OF CRITIC
MARCH 3rd 2016

From the mind of critic: "If blue skies are smiling upon us, will we realize it before the clouds return? If opportunities and possibilities are all around, will we see them before self-sabotage sets in? If the world is our oyster, are we forcing ourselves to be allergic to shellfish? Being honest about who we are, how we feel and what we want to accomplish is how we move forward. Being honest with ourselves however, entails getting rid of escape plans. Once we no longer avoid, ignore or pretend our issues don't exist, all that's left is how we feel, and how we view the world. This can be difficult for anybody, let alone for those of us who've been escaping for a long time. Processing our truth can be hard, but it's real, just like the smiling blue sky. Once we're open to who we truly are, we can breathe in the beauty that has always been there, and always will be. Honesty is an evolutionary policy." ☺

FROM THE MIND OF CRITIC
MARCH 4th 2016

From the mind of critic: "What's the point of fighting for a better future, if we want that future to include us not fighting? What's the point of struggling to make the next generation better, if we don't want them to struggle once they get better? Is there a point we reach where we completely change our way of thinking? A rebel not knowing what to do once they've won membership into the majority, is the same as us not knowing what to do when we've been fighting and struggling for so long, that we've forgotten how to live. We must prepare to live in a better world while we're working to improve it, so we don't get caught off guard. Life is a journey that's constantly changing and evolving. Being able to picture this better world and our place in it however, is the first step in not only bringing it into existence, but ensuring its sustainability. Fighting and struggling to improve our station in life isn't bad, as long as love and peace are our motivation to not fight and struggle anymore." ☺

FROM THE MIND OF CRITIC
MARCH 5th 2016

From the mind of critic: "If we're an angry Republican do we vote for Trump, just like if we're an angry Democrat do we vote for Sanders? If we aren't angry, do you vote for Rubio or Clinton? If we aren't angry, but thirsting for change like a cool drink of water in the desert, do we even vote at all? The argument of whether to make change from the outside of the inside has been raging for millennia. Being angry isn't bad, as long as it spawns positive action. The only problem is when we take action while we're still angry, only to realize later things didn't work out because we weren't thinking clearly. Look, I have candidates I support, as I am sure you do too. We're all angry at the way things are, but until we get past that anger and clearly, intellectually and plainly chart a course forward together, we better get used to presidential pissing contests. When we institute a better world based on love and respecting our fellow man, our politicians will respond in kind." ☺

FROM THE MIND OF CRITIC

MARCH 8th 2016

From the mind of critic: "When we let go of what doesn't serve us, is it a one-time process? Does it create a situation we think is out of sight, out of mind, and miraculously gone forever? Is this an accurate portrayal of the letting go process? Is it a figment of our imagination that waving a magic wand will make unneeded emotions go away forever? We all have things we could let go of which don't serve us, things that drag us down instead of build us up. Letting go is a healthy thing. We only have so much room in our minds, and have to make room for the positive by getting rid of the negative. Problems appear after we've let go, and things start creeping back. We have to constantly clean our emotional space, just like our physical space. When we clean our house it looks great for a while, but becomes dirty if we don't clean it again, same with our minds. Letting go is constant just like receiving. To keep the flow going, we must feed our soul." ☺

FROM THE MIND OF CRITIC

MARCH 9th 2016

From the mind of critic: "If a portion of the population says they won't vote for a candidate because they don't know them, is it because the media covers their opponent infinitely more? If the media then says that the population won't vote for the candidate because they don't know them, is it because their coverage barely mentions the candidate other than to say they're losing? If somebody is inherently anti-establishment, is it any wonder the establishment fights tooth and nail to stop them? This election season has brought to light many issues we've been struggling with, chief among them, money in politics and corporate media control. If people are hypocrites, then the politicians they create are hypocrites, and so are the media that covers them. Bernie can win and he will, once people start thinking for themselves, and stop having the media do it for them." ☺

FROM THE MIND OF CRITIC
MARCH 11th 2016

From the mind of critic: "If we want honest, fulfilling and purposeful lives, why do we keep electing politicians who are the opposite? If we as a vast majority disapprove of Congress but love our guy, is it because we can't admit there's a problem? Are we afraid of objectively looking at how the world actually is? None of us are perfect, and those of us who think we are, make the problem infinitely worse. Not being perfect and not being conscious are two totally different things. If we know something is an issue, we must speak up. Not saying what we think exacerbates every single problem we have. Not everybody will agree with or even like what we have to say, but we must converse, express and compromise if we hope to collectively evolve as a species. If we want to find what we're looking for, we have to be honest about an issue, solve it and then let it go. Do we want to authentically know joy and satisfaction?" ☺

FROM THE MIND OF CRITIC

MARCH 12th 2016

From the mind of critic: "When we say beware the ides of March, do we even know what the Ides of March means? Are we worried that something crazy is going to happen, or somebody is going to jump out of the shadows to get us? Are we frightened about the unknown, where our mind spins with a zillion possibilities at the same time? Change can be scary, but like death and taxes it has a high probability of happening. We can't control everything that happens, but we can control our reactions. Instead of trying to think of every variable at once, we need to focus on what brings us joy. Not only will this focus give us the motivation to carry on, but it will also keep us sane. We can think of the Ides of March as a big scary thing we can't do anything about, or we can realize it might be an unexpected opportunity to make us better than we ever imagined." ☺

FROM THE MIND OF CRITIC
MARCH 15th 2016

From the mind of critic: "If we all have dues to pay because we can't change the past, do those same dues change the future? Are the dues different because one is focused on what has already happened, and the other on what is going to happen? Are there dues for changing the present? Dues we pay, challenges we face or obstacles we have to overcome, whatever we call the concept, it describes the same concept of discovery. We're all on our own journeys, learning things that work and things that don't, things we can change, and things we can't. Once we're present in the moment by being honest and kind to ourselves, we'll see the past and the future are simply guides to make our present more fulfilling. If the dues we have to pay are merely being kind to ourselves, they aren't so imposing, are they?" ☺

FROM THE MINDOF CRITIC
MARCH 16th 2016

From the mind of critic: "If blue skies are smiling at us, is it a guarantee we'll always see blue skies? Is it a choice, where we decide to only see blue skies, and to ignore dark skies that may or may not be there? Is it a glimpse of what life could be like if we fully opened our eyes? Nice weather and warm temperatures can lift us out of the doldrums, if we think about what's ahead. Sometimes we can feel so locked into feeling down, that when somebody tries to lift us up, we push away because of our sardonic pleasure in not changing. Once we realize events, people and emotions will attempt to drag us down, we'll see that we feel better when we smile at blue sky as often as we can. Once we get used to smiling, we'll see that even if the sky is gray, we can always find something to smile at because our eyes and heart are open." ☺

FROM THE MIND OF CRITIC
MARCH 17th 2016

From the mind of critic: "Is it possible to get up on water skis by pulling the boat, or by letting the boat pull you? Is it possible to succeed in life by forcing it to happen, or by trusting the process and letting it work? Is the sheer will and determination we feel at the bottom of our soul, enough to change the known definition of what's possible? No matter how much effort, work, heartache, blood, sweat, tears and time we put into something, it's not guaranteed. Now the more work, preparation and research we put in creates a higher probability of success, but not a sure thing. Hell, with technology and loopholes, neither are death and taxes. Once we realize the work we put in is more effective when we let that work, work for us, we'll see that forcing something to happen negates all the work we put in, because we're saying it wasn't enough. There is no reason to prepare for something we plan on forcing. There is also every reason to believe our hard work will pay off if we allow it to. The boat of life will pull us whether we want it to or not, we might as well ski while it's happening." ☺

FROM THE MIND OF CRITIC
MARCH 18th 2016

From the mind of critic: "If we're America the beautiful like we claim, do we remember how to crown thy good with brotherhood from sea to shining sea? Does our brotherhood only include people who think, look and act like us? Do we comprehend the full definition of brotherhood, which includes brothers, sisters, animals and all other living things on the earth? We can claim all day that we're accepting of people, and as long as somebody has the courage and determination, their mind can help them achieve anything. However, if our actions are utterly detrimental, because we believe life, liberty and the pursuit of happiness only apply to us, and not those weirdly stinky people with strange beliefs, than we have no idea what brotherhood really means. We prove that we cherish brotherhood with our fellow man by not just talking the talk, but walking the walk. We stay American by continually taking steps forward." ☺

FROM THE MIND OF CRITIC
MARCH 19th 2016

From the mind of critic: "Are we an extension of our politics, or is our politics an extension of ourselves? What about religion, are we an extension of it, or is it an extension of ourselves? Are politics and religion so hard to talk about, because we can't admit that we're the reason politics and religion are so out of whack? If we really want to fix our political issues, and honestly want to see a future where we have a polite and kind discourse, we must look in the mirror. How we treat ourselves and those around us magnifies our soul with either lightness, or darkness. Disagreement is not only healthy, but the best part of our democracy because we can take part without fear of judicial killing. What isn't healthy is putting down others by undermining American values, then when people protest, we say it's because they disagree and want us silenced. People who claim they're the most American, and have to boast about it to everyone they meet, prove to the letter why they're the exact opposite. If we want to be authentic human beings, we must realize how we treat others, influences everything in the entire world." ☺

FROM THE MIND OF CRITIC

MARCH 24th 2016

From the mind of critic: "When we go to the polls do we vote for who we want as president, or who we want to see as President? Do we choose a candidate based on emotional reactions, or intellectual ones? Should we select a leader of the future, or a leader that changes the future? We're all familiar with the plethora of choices we have in this election, and at the crossroads where we've collectively arrived. Many of us are angry and want to make change. Some of us want to make change, but aren't angry. While the rest of us don't know or don't care, which spawns the rise of politicians telling us how to act and think. Do we want to think and then choose who represents all of us? Do we want somebody to do the thinking and choosing for us? Even though it's our choice and our choice alone, it affects everyone." ☺

FROM THE MIND OF CRITIC
MARCH 25th 2016

From the mind of critic: "If none of us succeed until we all succeed, do none of us fail until we all fail? Is failure the opposite side of the coin from success, or a different currency all together? Are success and failure subjective, and can change with each person and experience? We all live in an interconnected world that feeds off us as social beings. Some of us might gain money, power and influence, but are we truly successful if we push others down to get there? Some of us might fail over and over and over, but are we truly failures if we motivate others with our resilience, which in turn motivates us? Success and failure are relative, just as life is based on perception. How we see things and how we view the world, affects what we see as positive and negative. Just as failures aren't failures if we learn from them, successes aren't successes if we don't learn from them either. Life becomes clear when we step outside of ourselves to share with others, and becomes foggy when we keep it to ourselves. Our job is to figure out what leads to success, and what lead to failure, being open, or being closed?" ☺

FROM THE MIND OF CRITIC

MARCH 26th 2016

From the mind of critic: "If we have a two party system in this country, why do we allow third parties to run in elections? Is it because we know they have no reasonable chance to upset the status quo, which makes them the ultimate token gesture? Is it because Democrats and Republicans have been gaining money, power and influence for a long time, and can steamroll the small parties? Do the small parties have just as much right to run and grow, because they still view this as America? I've been a registered green party member for years, because their platform is the closest to my personal views. I've been voting Democrat, because their platforms are closest to mine, but actually have a chance at winning. We shouldn't have to pick the lesser of two evils. We should pick somebody who isn't evil, somebody who wants to build us up, and not tear us down. To be accountable to our fellow man like never before, why do we need political parties?" ☺

FROM THE MIND OF CRITIC
MARCH 29th 2016

From the mind of critic: "If we're trying to trust the process and let it work, have we figured out what our process is? Have we figured out what works and what doesn't, so we know what our process looks like? Is everything in life changing and evolving, making it impossible to identify a process? To figure out what works and what doesn't, we have to realize that our process will be different from our peers, but not totally alien. What works for us, might not work for somebody else and vice versa. That doesn't mean we aren't guiding our process toward the same basic place. It means that to identify our process, we have to ask ourselves the tough questions from which we've been shying away. What do we want, what do we need and when, where would we like to go, how are we going to get there, and why is it important? Once we answer these questions, our process will appear. We trust the process and let it work by letting words spawn action, not by gripping them to death." ☺

FROM THE MIND OF CRITIC
MARCH 30th 2016

From the mind of critic: "If we ask why not us or when is it going to be our time, are we stifling ourselves by asking the wrong questions? Are we inadvertently placing roadblocks in front of our progress because we're asking questions at all? Are wonder, hopes, wants and dreams helpful, until they turn into obsessions? Whether it's viewing somebody more successful, seeing somebody with a love we want or somebody with the drive that makes anything possible, it describes our anger about what we don't have, instead of graciousness for what we do. Being grateful for what we have is how we move forward, by giving us motivation to achieve our dreams. What if we're a lonely person who is getting older, and wants to share their love with somebody they truly connect with, and feel high just being around? Should we keep telling ourselves that it will happen one day, or the right one will come along when we least expect it, even if we've been telling ourselves the same thing for 20 years, and might have to for another 20? How can we be grateful for what we have, when we don't have what we truly want? We keep bettering ourselves, what else are we going to do?" ☺

FROM MIND OF CRITIC

MARCH 31st 2016

From the mind of critic: "If we beat loneliness by discovering how our life's purpose is integral to the collective evolution of the planet, does the authentic love we long for help or hinder? Does the planet know how important our work is, steering us away from love? Would the energy we need to work our passion and purpose, go towards that love we found, leaving nothing for our life's work? The energy expended with somebody we love and cherish, is the same energy we gain from working our dreams. Sometimes when we're searching for answers, we end up with more questions. We should always go after our dreams, regardless of if we've found love. Sometimes we can be so comfortable after we've found love, we stop searching for ways to better the planet, because we don't picture things getting any better. We must remember that true love will inspire us to grow, not stifle us into not growing in a direction we don't want to go. True love only adds to the quality of life, we're the ones that stifle ourselves. We control our own destiny, true love only adds to it." ☺

FROM THE MIND OF CRITIC
APRIL 1st 2016

From the mind of critic: "When prices rise for basic goods and necessities, is it because of a minimum wage hike? Do prices rise over time, no matter what wages levels are, because greed for more, more, more overtakes our critical thinking skills? Economic issues have passionate supporters on both sides. When prices rise, it effects people on the lower end, much more than people on the higher end. Statistics will show that when you give people on the bottom more money, they spend it back into the economy, at an exponentially higher rate than people at the top. Some of us will say raising wages will cause all prices to rise, and there will be fewer jobs and more layoffs because of it. This line never pans out in reality, because prices ALWAYS rise. Plus if that advice was actually heeded, we wouldn't have safety regulations, labor laws or labeling laws because they'd cause prices to rise as well. The economy has gotten better since 2008, but mostly for the top. When things get better for people at the bottom, it strengthens the middle class, which is the true barometer of an economy. If prices are going to rise anyway, shouldn't wages rise as well so we can afford those prices?" ☺

FROM THE MIND OF CRITIC
APRIL 2nd 2016

From the mind of critic: "If the wheel in the sky keeps on turning, and we don't know where we'll be tomorrow, what can we do today to make sure we're pointed in the right direction? What template or pallet will we construct so we have the best materials to pull from? Do our thoughts push our actions, or do our actions push our thoughts when we step into the unknown? Trying to get out of our own way is extremely difficult, when we see others so much further ahead. The grass is always greener on the other side, didn't appear as a saying out of thin air. We must remember people will be ahead of us, just as often as behind us. With us in the middle of this chaotic soup we call life, the best thing we can do is uplift our soul as often as possible. We do that by accepting what we need, and feeling gratitude for what we have. This will give us the motivation to keep focused when others try tearing us down, and especially when we tear ourselves down. The wheel in the sky will always turn, whether we turn with it or not. However, the unknown isn't nearly as scary if we prepare ourselves, by getting excited about all the great things to come." ☺

FROM THE MIND OF CRITIC

APRIL 5th 2016

From the mind of critic: "If there are way more of us than them, how come they insist on control in all their actions? Are "they" a monolithic group, made up of the same people who all want the same thing? Are "they" whoever "we" want them to be? Since life is what we make it, than "they", "we" and "us" can have different meanings depending on our life experience, political and religious views, and our emotional and physical state. Once we realize this, we'll see that "we", "they", "them", "us" and any other pronoun we come up with, are labels that don't mean anything, other than to make sense out of the chaos. A critical mass of people will always overpower a smaller group of people, no matter how powerfully that smaller group portray itself. The masses can make a difference against the elites, and will drive them in the direction that benefits the masses. Numbers lie, physical bodies don't." ☺

FROM THE MIND OF CRITIC
APRIL 6th 2016

From the mind of critic: "If the dreams that we dare to dream really do come true somewhere over the rainbow, is that also where the leprechaun lives? Is finding the pot of gold at the end of the rainbow, the same thing as having our dreams come true? Does using a metaphor with fictional attributes only make it harder to achieve our dreams? Does it make it sound like getting to a completely made up place, is the only place our real world dreams will come true? Beautiful words, sounds and images stir up joyful emotions, which give us the motivation to achieve our goals, hopes and dreams. They give us a window into what the universe wants us to be. Breathing in the beautiful images and energy is one thing, but believing our dreams will only come true after reaching a place that's totally fictional, is the biggest roadblock we can create. We must realize our dreams occur in front of our face when we put the work in, because we have the courage to allow ourselves to live them. Breathing the beauty of the world gives us the determination to do the work, but isn't THE work. Somewhere over the rainbow is a beautiful place, but we don't live there. To better our now, we have to be here now." ☺

FROM THE MIND OF CRITIC

APRIL 7th 2016

From the mind of critic: "Does the status quo only attack when they feel threatened? Do false claims, twisted words and outright lies abound when the establishment feels it's their only defense? Are all those attacks a projection of how they truly feel about themselves, or a fear of change the people are screaming at the top of their lungs that they want? A political campaign is the nastiest, dirtiest and most despicable thing human beings have ever come up with, but they don't have to be. Exaggerated and dehumanizing attacks have been around as long as elections, which means beating opponents into submission has woven itself into the culture. Do people attack when they aren't strong enough on their issues? Once we realize that if people can't run on what the majority of the populace wants, we'll see that they shouldn't be running in the first place. Too much money makes politics nothing more than a big fancy fundraiser, where politicians dance to the tune of whoever gives the most money, and only listens to their needs. When the money disappears, issues reappear. When we stop attacking each other, so will politicians. Until then, how about we choose the candidate that dances to nobody's tune, except the $27 donor?" ☺

FROM THE MIND OF CRITIC
APRIL 8th 2016

From the mind of critic: "Does pragmatism or extremism represent more of the population? Is it a mixture of both, where we like to solve problems but from an extreme perspective? Does pragmatism represent compromise, and extremism represent nihilism? We all have opinions, whether we choose to voice them or not. If we don't know enough about something to have an opinion, we have thoughts. Even if those thoughts are that we don't know anything, they're still thoughts. If we're truly convinced we don't have any thoughts, we're kidding ourselves. This gives us the proverbial blank slate, and an extremely fertile breeding ground for nihilism. When thoughts are introduced to this blank slate, they quickly become unbreakable opinions. When we've convinced ourselves that we don't know any better, extremism is formed. Once we see our opinions are no stronger or weaker than other's opinions, we can begin to fix our problems without compromising who we are. Balancing pragmatism and extremism will not only make us better humans, but will show us how our thoughts matter, and that we can make up our own mind. Critical thought done in an honest way is how we collectively save ourselves, specifically so we can collectively save the planet." ☺

FROM THE MIND OF CRITIC

APRIL 9th 2016

From the mind of critic: "If the most stimulating conversations happen with people we disagree with, how come we shy away from them? Is it because the tone, word choice and lack of evidence make the conversation devolve into personal attacks when the other party disagrees with us? Are we scared we'll be shown something we can't deny, that will flip our world upside down? If we ever hope to get past the issues we've convinced ourselves that we can't, we have to communicate. It isn't us versus them, it's us versus us. There's so much we can agree on, if we can past our own bullshit; that talking to each other like living, breathing and thinking humans trying to find joy in a chaotic world, will make us realize we're way more alike than we care to admit. If we start from love, peace, justice and brotherhood for our fellow man, we'll be less likely to lay personal attacks, because we'd be attacking ourselves. We don't have to hug it out, but we must talk it out. It's better than adding to the body count right? Disagreement as a concept is normal, fighting disagreement as a concept is not." ☺

FROM THE MIND OF CRITIC

APRIL 12th 2016

From the mind of critic: "If the world is changing, evolving and moving forward and we want to be part of it, can we ignore the voices of the younger generation, considering they're why we're evolving? Can we say in fact we want the same change the young people want just slower, when they say we're all hypocrites who talk out of both sides of our mouth? Has this "us versus them" mentality caused some of us to vote our fears, and some of us to vote our hopes? When young people say they want Wall Street out of politics and a candidate echoes the sentiment, then takes millions in contributions through super PACs, is it a wonder why young people call candidates hypocrites? Is it a wonder that same candidate has a 60% disapproval rating, and that the younger crowd favors their opponent 3-1? If we know the younger generation is constantly reshaping and reforming the status quo, we must hear them and work their solutions, or we'll get left behind." ☺

FROM THE MIND OF CRITIC
APRIL 13th 2016

From the mind of critic: "Will we ever learn to do something, if other people always do it for us? Do we expect to succeed and move forward, if we always assume people will do things for us? Do we truly not know how to do things, or do we know how, but want others to do them because it's beneath us, and don't want to be bothered? Within our job, our house, or any aspect of our daily routine, things have to happen whether we want them to or not. If we glide through life expecting others to pick up the slack, we're nothing but little floaties that drift along the river, which can disappear any moment. Our will to live dissipates when we have no idea who we are or what we want, because we've put no work in to find out; which is a great way to live if we dream to be a puppet or a politician. If we want to live life without somebody pulling our strings, we must put the work in. If we're ready to be real human beings, we must better ourselves by ourselves. If we want to pass the test of life, we can't cheat off somebody else's paper." ☺

FROM THE MIND OF CRITIC
APRIL 14th 2016

From the mind of critic: As candidates get anxious about their judgment day, is there any difference in pandering to party elites for their support, and pandering to the voters for theirs? If a candidate has honed their message to gain the support their opponent has garnered, isn't it the very definition of pandering? Is changing ones beliefs what politics is, or just what it's turned into? We're supposed to be a country that has a say in who its leaders are. Cynicism of leaders gets tremendously worse, when party bosses, surrogates and "super delegates" think they have just as much say as the people. Cynicism gets worse when 3/4 of a politicians time is spent raising money, and only 1/4 of their time doing their actual job. Cynicism reaches a fever pitch when the electorate is told to do as I say, not as I do. Not that I'd ever want a president Trump, because I definitely don't. However, we need somebody like him to run against somebody like Bernie if we ever hope to combat the cynicism that things will never change. Pandering stops being the norm in politics when we vote our wants and not our fears. Sanders vs. Trump is an accurate portrayal of where we're at, and where each side would like to go." ☺

FROM THE MIND OF CRITIC

APRIL 15th 2016

From the mind of critic: "If we're told lie after lie after lie, do we begin to believe them? If deflecting and doubling down are then utilized when we confront these lies, does it make us believe them? If the armor cracks when we lie, does the armor become stronger when we confront and ask follow up questions to our follow up questions? Whether we're politicians hiding our real views and positions, civilians lying about who we are and what we've done, or kids sneaking cookies out of the cookie jar, it all describes trying to get away with something. This need comes from portraying ourselves as something were not, because we think people won't like the real us. This false portrayal can cause us to go after things which bring us short term happiness, but long term dread, anger and sadness about what we don't have. If we're an elected official, we might pander to all groups we believe support us, while doing whatever the hell we want. Lying and deflecting only gets worse when we become politicians. If we can stop the cycle early on, we should. In the end Republicans will vote for Republicans not Democrat light, and Democrats will vote for Democrats, not Republican light. Whatever side of the political spectrum we find ourselves on, the more we vote for somebody who actually represents us, the more we'll get somebody who actually represents us." ☺

FROM THE MIND OF CRITIC
APRIL 16th 2016

From the mind of critic: "Near the end of an increasingly heated campaign, does the amount of candidates, surrogates and supporters that sell fear go up? Do voters flock around the candidate they fear least? Does the average person see through the propagandic fog, because they realize an election isn't a pissing contest over who can make the world sound scarier? How many times have we had to choose between the lesser of two evils? After we learn the concept of fear sold to the highest bidder, we see elections are the evil of two lessers. Maybe our system has gotten so corrupted by the ultra-rich, that we vote for the less worse. Maybe we've gotten so desensitized to the vitriol and hate, that we don't pay attention to elections. Greatly reduced voting numbers, causes candidates to sell fear to the few voters remaining, because they know a bigger crowd would never put up with it. Fear is a normal human emotion. However, when we let it overrun our critical thinking skills, big money interests seize the opportunity like sharks to blood in the water. We don't fix problems by being scared of how bad they are. We fix problems by remembering how good we are." ☺

FROM THE MIND OF CRITIC

APRIL 19th 2016

From the mind of critic: "If we set goals by putting out to the universe what we want, and back them up by preparing and doing the work required, what do we do if we don't succeed? Do we give up because the success we thought meant for us, was really meant for somebody else? Do we adjust our strategy because of changing landscapes and environments, and our ever evolving collective consciousness? Thomas Edison failed several thousand times before he perfected the light bulb. He never gave up. He kept tweaking his strategy until he achieved success. Edison knew his idea would eventually work, because he knew in his heart it would. In that, he never saw himself failing, just not succeeding yet. Same with us, we need hopes, dreams and goals to feel like we matter. We need to put the work in so we're in the best position to succeed. Once we feel like we matter, we can adjust whatever and whenever so we can accomplish what we want to accomplish. We can't let jerky people or our jerky selves stop us, by droning on about everything we need to change. Success is always attainable, we just might need to change our strategy. Is this the definition of keeping our eyes on the prize?" ☺

FROM THE MIND OF CRITIC
APRIL 20th 2016

From the mind of critic: "As we move closer to a battle between Democrats, Republicans and token third parties, will the same old saga prove that the 2 party system has outlived its usefulness? Have elections become so pointless to the next generation, because they see how political parties aren't equally represented in news coverage and debates? Are people finally prepared to ask why we need political parties at all? We've all gotten sick because of the overwhelming glut of money in politics, making it easier for the elites to maintain control. Why else would we need political parties other than to give money and support to our candidates? What else do they really do? People running for office could build their own organization, fundraising apparatus and get out the vote efforts. Some of us might say well, why don't we take many candidates with the same basic ideas and unite them, so they're stronger than the people they fundamentally disagree with? The problem is if we spend all our time fighting the other side, how can we ever hope to unite? We should vote for a candidate who talks about issues we care about, not for the party that supports them. Political parties only cater to big money people, and those of us who don't pay attention. Political parties are an appendix, sometimes you have to rip them out to preserve the health of the body." ☺

FROM THE MIND OF CRITIC
APRIL 21st 2016

From the mind of critic: "If we want to stop taking advantage of each other, do we simply treat each other how we'd like to be treated? If we want people to stop taking advantage of us, do we treat them with kindness because we know their schemes, scams, anger and projection toward us stems from an intensely low self-esteem? Can we begin our day by telling ourselves we are good enough, so it permeates all our daily interactions? When somebody puts us down it can be hard to endure. We want to defend ourselves because we don't like how it makes us feel. This is a normal reaction, but it doesn't mean we can't evolve past it. Instead of instantly going on the defensive, we could see the fear and low self-esteem being pushed on us, and empathize because we've been there. This is where we begin to treat others like we'd like to be treated, because we see how our attitudes affect other's attitudes, and the next people they interact with and so on. Empathy and humanism are extremely contagious. They're the key to our collective evolution because they provide the love we require as humans. We learn many things in life, but what we learned in kindergarten is the key to enlightenment." ☺

FROM THE MIND OF CRITIC
APRIL 22nd 2016

From the mind of critic: "If we want to light a BBQ in the rain, are we crazy? Is it because our oven, stove and microwave are down, and we have no other way to make dinner? Is it because we really love BBQ? There is something very freeing about saying fuck it, I'm going to do something no matter how impossible it seems. Something changes when we stop listening to others tell us we can't do something, and start hearing ourselves admit we can. We have infinitely more ability than we give ourselves credit for. This conscious talent is unleashed on the world when we stop doing what's probable, and start doing what's possible. Roadblocks are difficult to get around until we realize they're imaginary, and have no hold over us unless we let them. Nothing can stop us from achieving. Hard work is hard, but becomes much easier when it moves us closer toward our hopes and dreams. Lighting a BBQ in the rain can be difficult, but the food will be the best damn thing we ever tasted." ☺

FROM THE MIND OF CRITIC

APRIL 23rd 2016

From the mind of critic: "Should a higher population center have more of a say than a lower population center in how society should run? Should the majority give the minority guidelines on how to live? Does equal representation require every person to have an equal voice, vote and influence, period? Areas with millions of people shouldn't tell areas with hundreds of people what to do, and vice versa. The issues that drag us down are the same no matter where we live, and so are the ways we can prosper. United we stand and divided we fall is a cliché, because it's the ultimate advice in moving forward. Whether we have one congressman of fifty, we all have two senators. Which is one small token of coming together, but we can do sooooooooooo much more. Us versus them has never worked and will never work, because all the fighting and battling will cause us to die sooner, our resources to dwindle faster, and will cause us to believe the world is coming to end, so there's no need to fix it. Coming together to fix the world requires numbers, which means people everywhere lending a hand. We collectively evolve by treating others how we'd like to be treated." ☺

FROM THE MIND OF CRITIC
APRIL 26th 2016

From the mind of critic: "As we head into another big election night, do we all care enough to vote? If we complain until the cows come home, are we ready to do something about it? Do we think complaining is acting, so we don't have to do anything else? Everybody has excuses and opinions about who they want as president, who they don't want, and why they may or may not care. Not caring and complaining are both inaction, because they put the actions out there for somebody else to do. Once we realize all action is thinking, feeling and complaining, followed up by vigilant attention to facts, backgrounds and sustained pressure on public officials, we'll see that voting is how we keep our president accountable, along with the courts, congress and military. We need a multi-pronged approach. We need to vote, but we also need to change our system so our leaders represent us, and not their fundraisers who they spend 80% of their day talking to. It all boils down to a question. Do we care about others, or only about ourselves? If we don't care about what's going on, we shouldn't care when we get screwed over." ☺

FROM THE MIND OF CRITIC

APRIL 27th 2016

From the mind of critic: "When we support something, does our support wane when a different option appears to have a better chance at success? If we support a candidate because they support an issue, how can we support the other candidate when they think that issue doesn't affect them? How can we be expected to abandon our beliefs because one side is less scary than the other? When both parties support their version of fear, shouldn't hope and progress win out? I'm not proclaiming myself Bernie or bust, mostly because it's a label, and much like other labels they control and constrict. When one side gives a position, and then the other side gives the same position just to gain votes, doesn't that prove they don't really believe it? Doesn't that prove they'll say anything to anybody? How can we be scared into supporting a candidate, when we don't support them specifically because we aren't scared? It looks like it's coming down to a choice between an untrustworthy liar and a crazy person. Have we devolved so much into thinking that they're the only candidates to choose from? Have we completely forgotten about hope and progress?" ☺

FROM THE MIND OF CRITIC

APRIL 28th 2016

From the mind of critic: "If we spend time learning our principles, what do we do when we're asked to compromise? Do we flat out refuse, because we'd never go against what we stand for? Do we realize bigger and more expansive problems exist, and aren't always about us? I don't think we'd have a problem with compromising, if we knew we didn't have to give up our principles. I don't think we'd have a problem with paying taxes, if we saw something tangible come from them. When we do something we don't want to do, we want to get something out of it. Yes, getting our opposition do something we don't want to do is good, but isn't sustainable. Once we realize that true compromise is giving up some of what we want, to get some of what we want, we'll see all the magnitude of fakery out there portraying itself as compromise. Strategy and action are compromise, not promises and platitudes. Whether it's an untrustworthy liar, a crazy and racist flim-flam man, or a socialist Jew, we must move forward and evolve." ☺

FROM THE MIND OF CRITIC
APRIL 29th 2016

From the mind of critic: "Does determination and courage outweigh talent and education? If we aren't the smartest or strongest person in the room but we keep striving, moving, fighting, loving and evolving to move forward, will we succeed more than somebody who has all the talent and education in the world, but doesn't try? If we focus our minds in the right direction, do we have a much better chance at a joyful journey? Success is a journey and not a destination is the most overused and misinterpreted cliché in our repertoire. Many of us expend so much time trying to get to a place where we think we don't have to struggle, where we think things will come easy. This complacency keeps us from achieving success, and from striving for more. Once we realize that putting ourselves in the right place at the right time without knowing it, means being grateful, kind and open to learning, we'll see our journey's path light up. Complacency and apathy are enemies of success, and courage and determination are its drivers. Our job is to figure out what our process is, and then act on it. That's our journey." ☺

FROM THE MIND OF CRITIC

APRIL 30th 2016

From the mind of critic: "When life gives us lemons, we know we should make lemonade, but what if we've run out of sugar? Can we just run down to the store and buy more? Do we have to plant the seeds, nurture them and be happy when they start producing because we've manufactured our own? Making the best out of a bad situation is a concept we all should know. Sometimes however, we forget or misplace the positivity required to carry it out. Sure, we can purchase this positivity, a short lived fleeting happiness that gives off the aura of positivity, but floats away quickly because we didn't create it. If we cultivate positivity ourselves, it will last infinitely longer because it's the soul rejuvenating joy for which we've been searching. We'll also see that breathing in the immense beauty of the world all around us, introduces immense positivity whenever we need it. Life can be one big lemon sometimes, but once we see the sugar all around us, we'll truly understand that life isn't as sour as we think." ☺

FROM THE MIND OF CRITIC

MAY 3rd 2016

From the mind of critic: "Whether we think the poor take more advantage of the welfare state or that the rich take more advantage, does it have to do with our income level? If we believe immigration and citizenship requirements are too strict, and the cause of people coming over the border, or we believe that it's too easy to come here, and that we give the immigrants all this free stuff they don't have to pay for, does it have anything to do with us being an immigrant? Does having a certain life experience, guarantee the way we think about others having that experience? If it doesn't, how do fields like sociology spring up? Life is basically chaos, and we come up with all sorts of methods to make sense of that chaos. The best thing we can do is never commit black and white thinking. Once we stop believing all problems have a one size fits all solution, we'll see that what brings us joy and fulfillment isn't the same for others, so how could our thoughts be the same? Whether its immigration or welfare, no two people have the exact same opinions, so how could two people have the same motivations? Are we psychic, ignorant or critical self-thinkers?" ☺

FROM THE MIND OF CRITIC
MAY 4th 2016

From the mind of critic: "Are pragmatism and capitulation different concepts, like compromise and nihilism? Are they the same concepts, just using different labels like lawyers and attorneys? Is compromise necessary when confronting evil? If we've watched the Republican Congress at all, we'd know they think compromise is blasphemy. Do the Democrats feel the same way? Is there a way to compromise without giving up on principles? Maybe I'm just having a hard time because I really, really, really don't like Hillary Clinton. Maybe I'm scared of the possible nuclear world war under Trump? Maybe, just maybe I'm angry that Bernie hasn't gotten nearly the amount of news coverage he deserves. The fact remains that Super Delegates don't vote until the convention. If Hillary goes over the 2300 mark with super delegates before the convention, it doesn't clinch anything. None of the networks are asking, what if Bernie wins all the remaining States, picks up delegates, and prevents Hillary from clinching with pledged delegates alone? How would a contested convention play out considering Bernie beats Hillary in every single national poll against Trump? This has become not a question of pragmatism and compromise, but one of fear of the future. Are we going to finally deal with it, or kick the can down the road once again?" ☺

FROM THE MIND OF CRITIC

MAY 5th 2016

From the mind of critic: "if we can't change every outcome but we can change our reaction, does that reaction in and of itself change the outcome? If we change our reaction, isn't that changing our perception? If we change our perception, don't we also change the outcome because we're changing the way we see it? We can only control how we feel, nobody else. Most people are going to do whatever they want to do no matter what we say. Once we realize the best way to move forward and leave our mark on the world is to be as authentic as we can, we'll see that our reactions are our actions, and we can make them negative or positive. We change the world, by changing ourselves. We can achieve what we've always dreamed of, we just have to be honest." ☺

FROM THE MIND OF CRITIC
MAY 6th 2016

From the mind of critic: "If there's no time like the present, then what's the point of thinking about the future? What's to say the past wasn't great? Are we supposed to use the past and the future to influence the present? Staying present and in the moment, is what keeps us glued to what's going on. We can worry about the future, but it will only make us not live up to our true potential, same with worrying about the past. We might never know the full breadth of our true potential. What we do know, is learning the lessons of the past so we don't repeat mistakes, and visualizing what we want for the future, makes our present worthwhile. Learning and letting go will surely make our present more stimulating and engrossing, and will prove the balance we're all trying to achieve. None of us want to be unbalanced in our present, right?" ☺

FROM THE MIND OF CRITIC

MAY 7th 2016

From the mind of critic: "If we all want to leave a mark, how do we want to be remembered and by who? Do we want to be remembered for all the good we did, and the marks we left in our attempts to make the world just a little bit better? Do we want to be remembered for all the bad we did, and the marks we left in our attempt to screw up the world by taking advantage of everybody and everything? The sooner we start thinking about how we want to be remembered, the sooner we'll see how it influences our actions. Everything we do is an opportunity to bring love and light to all people, even those who don't know the meaning of love and light. We spread good energy to them, and they spread good energy to everybody they know and so on. What we come to realize after trial and error, is that bad energy can spread just as fast as good energy, and in the same way. The mark we leave is equal to the energy we put out. We just have to ask ourselves if bad or good energy is more fulfilling." ☺

FROM THE MIND OF CRITIC
MAY 10th 2016

From the mind of critic: "If we ever feel like everybody's trash man, do we neglect our own garbage? Do we begin thinking that cleaning up others garbage is easier than dealing our own, because we don't have to take responsibility? Do we realize always cleaning up others garbage, takes away from time we should be spending on ourselves? Sometimes we get so pissed off at what others do, it makes us blind to what we do. When other people make mistakes that we think are so obvious, it can make us think the world is coming to an end because it's overflowing with stupid people. Once we realize there will always be stupid people doing stupid things no matter what we do or say, we'll see that there's no point in getting upset if it's going to happen anyway, so we might as well do what we need to do for us. Picking up garbage can get old when it's not ours. If we pick up our own garbage, we'll have peace of mind that we took care of ourselves. We must take care of ourselves, specifically before we take care of others." ☺

FROM THE MIND OF CRITIC

MAY 11th 2016

From the mind of critic: "If we've all been told that if we don't have anything nice to say we shouldn't say it at all, what do we do when somebody says something not constructive? Do the same rules apply? Is it all part of the same concept, because saying something nice and saying something constructive are both meant to improve the person they're directed at? In an effort to get us to be kind to each other, we've been told we should say nice things to each other. Which is good as long as we aren't ignoring underlying problems, by saying things that aren't constructive. Once we realize constructive comments are better than ignoring or saying something mean, we'll see that when we have somebody else's best interest at heart, we only want them to grow and evolve into a better person just like we want for ourselves. If constructive comments come from a place of love and light, they can be the deepest way of being nice. As long as it's not the only thing we focus on when interacting with somebody, they'll hear us. We all grow, improve and evolve only when we help each other grow, improve and evolve." ☺

FROM THE MIND OF CRITIC
MAY 12th 2016

From the mind of critic: "If we don't know where we're going until we get there, is there a guide book to point us in the right direction? Is this guide book the same for all seven billion people on earth? Are there infinite guide books written in infinite languages, but whose end goals are all pretty much the same? Many of us go through the same issues when trying to bring ourselves joy and fulfillment. We don't know where or what this joy and fulfillment is, we just know that we want it yesterday. This is when we look for signs, symbols, guides and sages. They could come in the form of the Bible, the Torah, the Quran, the Bhagavad-Gita, the Book of the Dead, the unwritten book of the road, or anything written, unwritten, spoken or implied that we encounter. Once we realize it doesn't matter what reaches us or in what form just that we're reached, we'll see that putting somebody down for what they believe in, is like saying we deserve inner joy more than them because our path is better. In the end, it doesn't matter how we find our way to inner joy, just that we do, and we help others find their way as well. As long as we stay open, we will find our way." ☺

FROM THE MIND OF CRITIC

MAY 13th 2016

From the mind of critic: "If we believe half of what we see and none of what we hear, how can we be told anything that'll change our minds for the better? Can we be shown something half of the time that will still make a difference? Does the fact that half of everything we see on a daily basis might be bullshit, create blinders as we attempt to evolve? There's a lot of truth in the concept of not buying into everything that comes along. Impossible to satiate Elites are always looking for their next mark, so we must be careful. We can't let ourselves think everybody is out to take advantage of us, because it blocks all good people and good messages. If we completely block everything we're taking the easy way out, because we're too lazy to decipher what's good and what's bad. Picking through everything to keep the good and leave the bad might be hard, but is extremely rewarding because it's authentic. It's not about believing none of what we hear and half of what we see. It's about not taking anything personally until we figure out if it helps or hurts our journey. We want to keep journeying right?" ☺

FROM THE MIND OF CRITIC

MAY 14th 2016

From the mind of critic: "Are we about to enter the "summer" of our discontent, because we've predetermined the outcome? Have we prepared ourselves for a series of bad events, practically willing them to occur? Has the confidence of an optimistic outcome, become overshadowed by a festering negativity? Have thoughts of our collective humanity's potential been fogged over? A lot of negativity can enter our thinking, because of the way certain life experiences have occurred. Maybe we got a raw deal. Maybe we've been persecuted. Maybe drama is drawn to us. Maybe our governmental structure has been shunning everyone that's not a billion dollar donor. Maybe they aren't paying attention to us, because they try to prove on a 24-7 basis, that we have no voice. Once we realize that when our perception changes, so does the amount of time we wallow in negativity, we'll see that this doesn't have to be the "summer" of our discontent, it could be the summer of contentment. That is, if being content is actually our goal." ☺

FROM THE MIND OF CRITIC

MAY 17th 2016

From the mind of critic: "If we took care of what we're supposed to, do we wait for others to do what they're supposed to? If we take care of other people, do some then feel like they don't have to? Are there simply drifters, floaters and doers in life, and to expect anybody to change is like waiting for pigs to fly? Many, many things in life stress us out, piss us off and throw us so off balance that it's extremely hard to deal with. It can be a person doing something we'd ever think of doing, or don't deem acceptable. We must realize events and people will always piss us off, we just can't let them get to us. How do we do that? We keep bettering ourselves, and putting energy into our passion. Once we get used to how that feels, stupid, complacent and apathetic people won't get to us as much. We'll always have to deal with them, but our turnaround time will be much shorter. We must focus on what's important to us, not what some apathetic person thinks is important to them." ☺

FROM THE MIND OF CRITIC

MAY 18th 2016

From the mind of critic: "When we see people make mistake after mistake, which gets excused every time we point them out, how do we keep our sanity? How can we be the best people we can be, when people are screwing up left and right with no consequences? Do we act like nothing happened? Do we talk about mistakes so incessantly that people become more upset at us, than the people who screwed up in the first place? All of us have trials and tribulations, which make up the plethora of chaos that we are as humans. Some of us are just better at dealing with this chaos than others. Some of us expect others to deal with our mistakes, so we can keep living in ignorance. Some us don't parasite on the backs of others, because the idea of pawning our shit off isn't in our psyche. We must realize that not being called out, hinders our collective evolution. How do we wake up? We wake up by realizing somebody won't always be there to wipe our ass. If we ever want to get ahead, we better learn how to wipe ourselves." ☺

FROM THE MIND OF CRITIC

MAY 19th 2016

From the mind of critic: "If united we stand and divided we fall is true, how come we get so fired up when detailing our differences, that division is the only possible outcome? Do we think the only way we can unite, is if the other side comes around to our side? Do we know compromise isn't a dirty word, and doesn't mean we have to compromise what we believe in? At no other time are we more divided than election time. By definition we pick sides, and vote for the person we think will do the best job. Things get interesting when we spend an eighteen month period denigrating, attacking and putting down somebody we see as our opponent, and then we're expected to come together. I'm not even talking about the volume of corruption it takes to anoint a nominee, which has been the case since Democratic super delegates were created. Is it even possible to stand together, when every dirty and underhanded tool is used to divide our loyalties? Unification is possible if we stop tearing down the other side, and instead highlight where we already agree. Of course if we did that, why would we need political parties at all?" ☺

FROM THE MIND OF CRITIC

MAY 20th 2016

From the mind of critic: "Do labels help us make sense out of chaos, or do they keep us ignorant to what's really happening? Are labels what we use to describe what we're thinking about? Do we use labels to write off the ravings of yet one more lunatic, somebody who is simply not as good as us? Whether its political parties, sociological studies, or just laziness and ignorance, labels squeeze us into a neat and tidy, black and white box. While this might hone the chaos into a digestible morsel, it sets us on a path headed in the wrong direction. Life is always morphing and evolving. Labels only serve to stop life's journey in its tracks. Political parties are useless, they prevent us from realizing that if a candidate wanted to run on issues they cared about, they could build a movement themselves. Sociology is useless because its studies are based on generalizations, which always feature exceptions and anomalies. Labels help us make sense of what we see, or keep us ignorant. We just have to ask ourselves, do we want the easy but ignorant path, or the challenging but fulfilling path?" ☺

FROM THE MIND OF CRITIC

MAY 21st 2016

From the mind of critic: "Does persecution and subjugation cause those of us with low self-esteem to control others, because we can't control ourselves? Is this lack of control due to ignorance? Does the control we seek, spawn from never having somebody school us on how everybody is the same, but different at the same time? This country and the world, has a long history of persecuting what we don't know as the "other", "exotic" and "strange". While it's true that life is a journey of evolving comprehension, it's also true that we'll be presented with people, places and things which challenge our preconceived notions. How we react to these challenges, is equal to the amount of vitriol we spew at the "other" and the "weirdo". While we can't control the challenges that come our way as we journey, we can control our reactions. Once we realize treating others how we'd like to be treated isn't just a rule for kindergartners but adults too, we'll see that we should never subjugate somebody else, because we'd be subjugating ourselves. We raise the world's self-esteem, by raising our own self esteem." ☺

FROM THE MIND OF CRITIC
MAY 24th 2016

From the mind of critic: "If we've spent a lot of time manifesting what we want by being open to opportunities which haven't happened yet, should we give up? Should we adjust what we want, so there is less to manifest? Do we have to spend more time energizing our soul, so we have the stamina to keep plugging away? All of us have goals, dreams and aspirations of bringing ourselves joy, and making our lives more fulfilling. Whether it's to be wildly successful in a chosen career, finding the love connection that makes our soul sing, or helping to further conscious evolution, manifesting what we want is very useful. It is however only one tool among many, which might not work as well as they once did, but that doesn't mean we stop using tools. Once we realize positivity breeds positivity, and negativity breeds negativity, we'll see that the more positive and happy we are, the more likely we are to manifest what we want. We can't always control outcomes, but we can control preparation. Energizing our soul is necessary for manifesting anything, which requires preparation. We can't give up, or we'd be saying we don't deserve it." ☺

FROM THE MIND OF CRITIC

MAY 25th 2016

From the mind of critic: "If rules, regulations and laws are created by voting for somebody, who votes for somebody who votes for somebody, who then votes after they appoint a staff to write the law, do we really have a say in the process? Do those of us who hold power use this confusion to act with impunity? Do the rest of us fight each other over who has more control, when really it's been taken from all of us? Do we see through the propaganda storm to form our own thoughts and opinions not because we belong to a group, but because we're human beings who can think for ourselves? United we stand and divided we fall has been used a million times. If we're all witnesses to the top screwing us over, but can't agree on how fast or how hard because we never ask why, we'll always be screwed over. The question "why", is the most important question in the English language. Without it, we'd be screwed over and over again because we wouldn't question. Isn't that how things are now? If all of us asked why more often, we would unite because we'd see that we agree on most things. Rules and laws would actually matter if they protected the entire population, not just the top 1/10th of 1%." ☺

FROM THE MIND OF CRITIC
MAY 26th 2016

From the mind of critic: "If our light is on but nobody's home, where did we go? Did we used to be home with the light on, but something caught our attention, causing us to run out the door without thinking? Are we home, but asleep? We've all heard that old saying before, and we all know what it's like to be here, but not really be here. It's like we're doing a task which requires our attention, but our mind is somewhere else. In that definition however, the main point gets lost. Our light is always on whether we're home or not. Sometimes we're home and take full advantage of our light, and everything it has to offer. Sometimes we're home and forget our light is on, because the darkness is too powerful. Sometimes we convince ourselves our light was never there, making the whole idea of finding our light a foreign concept. Once we realize our light burns forever, and can only be extinguished if we let it, we'll see that no matter how much we pretend light isn't there, our light is always there. It's there whether we want to believe it or not. All of our inner Tom Bodetts' have left our light on, but it's our choice to utilize light to better everything we are." ☺

FROM THE MIND OF CRITIC

MAY 27th 2016

From the mind of critic: "When life doesn't go as planned, do we just say fuck it and go home? Do we forget everything we've learned and blindly follow new found wisdom? Do we understand lessons we've learned, and use our knowledge to adapt in a way that benefits us and everybody in our circle? When unexpected challenges suddenly arise to throw our routine out the window, it tests our fortitude for life. Whether it's rolling with the punches, making the best out of a bad situation, expecting the unexpected or making lemonade out of lemons, it all describes the same concept. More than likely some version of our fight or flight response will be initiated, causing blueprints for the future to be designed. Once we realize that our choices can edit these blueprints, we'll see we benefit from change by realizing we have the ability to surprise ourselves. Yes everything is changing, and life will never be the same as it used to be. These changes can make us more conscious than we ever imagined, we just have to give our consent. Plans might help make sense out of the chaos, but will create more chaos if we're never willing to waver from them." ☺

FROM THE MIND OF CRITIC

MAY 28th 2016

From the mind of critic: "if we're lucky enough to have opened our souls to the beauty of the world, what do we do with the tidal wave of energy which results? If we use the energy toward our life's passions, what do we do with the wave of energy that comes directly from working our passion? How do we deal with the emotional roller coaster that follows as we try to keep the good energy flowing? When we spend time doing what we truly love, there's an amazing feeling that follows. This feeling opens us up to all the beauty, but also all the ugly feelings and thoughts we may have suppressed as a coping mechanism. Being open is being open, to the good and the bad. We can never be open to only one side, or we're not truly open. Once we realize that no matter how much good energy we breathe in, we can't totally erase our self-deprecating thoughts we can only minimize their importance, we'll see the act of breathing in good energy helps us decide what truly drives us, but we still have to decide. If life comes down to choices, will we tear ourselves down, or build ourselves up?" ☺

FROM THE MIND OF CRITIC

JUNE 2nd 2016

From the mind of critic: "If all we need to know we learned in kindergarten, can we just chill because we're done learning? Can we just float through life, because any knowledge that comes through is redundant? Does learning evolve over time, making the things we learned in kindergarten a foundation that knowledge builds on as we go through life? If we grew up in the 70s, 80s, or 90s, chances are we saw the poster promoting all the lessons we learned before entering grade school. This sentiment was designed to promote the idea of getting back to basics, remembering to share, treating others how we'd like to be treated, being kind and being honest. Now that we're older and entrenched in all the complexities of life in the 21st century, sometimes we forget about the basics, and then wonder why we aren't happy, can't find what we're passionate about, and can't find somebody to love. To create a life worth living, like a house, we need a strong foundation. Being kind to others, being honest and treating others as ourselves, puts us on track to build each other up, not tear each other down. We just have to ask what bring us joy, knowledge and consciousness, or ignorance and disassociation?" ☺

FROM THE MIND OF CRITIC

JUNE 3rd 2016

From the mind of critic: "When we say take care to somebody when we end an interaction, do we know the full meaning of the phrase? Do we blindly use the phrase because we're trying to be nice? Do we genuinely want people to take care of themselves, because we know the benefits for them, and everybody they come into contact with? We say a lot of things during the day we may or may not mean. Some things are so ingrained in our language and culture, that we say them without thinking; which portrays a larger problem within our species of talking without thinking. Many wars, skirmishes, and generational issues have festered simply because we didn't think before words came out of our mouths. Once we realize that we've said just as many bad things without thinking as good things, we'll see that we've been wishing others would take care of themselves for a long time. When we use the smallest amount of heart feeling when talking to people, many ingrained problems can be avoided. Being human to each other works much better when it's not just something to say, but something we actually feel, specifically because we've thought about it." ☺

FROM THE MIND OF CRITIC

JUNE 4th 2016

From the mind of critic: "When a well-known champion of human rights passes away, do we mourn their death by feeling an intense sadness that we didn't live out their world vision? Must we force ourselves to forget all the things they dreamed of? Must we remember all the great things they did, and all the great things they wanted to do, and use that to carry on their legacy to an even higher evolutionary place? Life can be sad and depressing when somebody who loved humanity is taken from us. We remember all the great things they accomplished. How they stood up against oppression and unjust war. How they stood up for religious freedom in a way that doesn't take rights and services away from people, but enhances them. How they stood up for loving thy neighbor, and not profiling, ridiculing, persecuting, violating, de-legitimizing, and hating thy neighbor. We remember all that and must realize, they were a conduit for our conscious and collective evolution, and so can we conduits in every interaction we have. We can stand up or humanity just as much as our beloved historical figures. When we do, we're proving their examples mean something. All of us can carry on when we listen to our own humanity." ☺

FROM THE MIND OF CRITIC
JUNE 7th 2016

From the mind of critic: "As the last big chunk of states vote today, will we be satisfied enough with the results to concede victory if we lose? Are we going to look at the results knowing they've been rigged and skewed toward the establishment, but view the other side as so evil, that we forget our convictions because fear of the other side has been drummed up by that same establishment? Are we going to fight on, keep moving, point out corruption whenever we see it, propose rule changes, and battle a system that will fight tooth and nail to hang onto power? The establishment has been behind Hillary since before day one. Most super delegates pledged their support for her, before any other candidate announced they were running. Corruption can be blinding and bias can be overwhelming, but the truth will win out if it's taken to heart. We the people are tired of voting for the evil of two lessers. We want truth, loyalty, and somebody who means what they say, not somebody who changes depending on who they're talking to. We want somebody who speaks truth to power, and somebody who in every poll taken beats Biff Tannon handily. We can beat Biff, if we don't concede to corruption." ☺

FROM THE MIND OF CRITIC

JUNE 8th 2016

From the mind of critic: "If we put our heart and soul into a candidate and they come up short, how are we supposed to throw our support behind another candidate when they represent everything that's wrong with the system, spelling out to the letter why we supported our original candidate in the first place? Are we supposed to forget all the reasons we liked our candidate when their opponent only paid them lip service? Do we fight for our rights and beliefs, and upend a system meant to steamroll everything we liked about our guy? None of us like losing when our heart and soul is invested. None of us like losing to a winner who garners support not by pulling on the loser's ideas, but by saying there's more that unites us than divides us. Basically saying we agree and the debate has been good, then not evoking one word about implementing some of the loser's ideas. Bernie is a great man, but Hillary and Trump spew platitudes with no substance. We move forward by making change now, not later. Can we get to the light now, or eventually? We the people know bullshit when we see it, and know when the system doesn't smell right." ☺

FROM THE MIND OF CRITIC
JUNE 9th 2016

From the mind of critic: "If honesty is the best policy and trust is the most important thing in any relationship, why do we keep electing people who are devoid of authenticity? Do candidates create a fake image to sell to their voters, while portraying a different image to their funders? Is the fakeness not a portrayal, but a normal outcropping of being scared to tell people what we really think? There's no wonder most of our politicians are full of shit, because most of us are full of shit. Since politicians come from us and how we collectively think, it's no wonder we can't believe anything they say. It's hard to trust people when we've been hurt and lied to so many times, that it's easy to be cynical. No matter what we convince ourselves of, there are good people out there. We just have to find the kernel amongst the shit. How we do that, is by being honest about who we are, and what we're looking for. We'll stop electing politicians who are liars and thieves, when we stop accepting ourselves as liars and thieves. We have to be the change we want to see, by acting on what we know is right." ☺

FROM THE MIND OF CRITIC

JUNE 10th 2016

From the mind of critic: "If we all want to leave a mark on the world, what are we doing to ensure that happens? Are we expecting to be remembered simply for being alive? Do we hope our hard work toward our passion pays off, and the world's collective consciousness slightly rises? We all want to be remembered, and we all want to matter. Many of us have a great fear that we'll be forgotten, and any memory of us will blow away like a feather in the wind. We combat this by finding something we can put our heart energy into. It's harder to combat fear when we haven't found our passion, and seem to be floating through life. That's not to say people who have found their passion are guaranteed to take meaningful steps through life. We all need to remember what's important to us, what matters and what brings us joy. If we put our heart energy into that, we're taking meaningful steps to realizing our passion. We all matter and we all count no matter what we accomplish because we're human. We leave a positive mark, when we put our heart energy into doing the right thing." ☺

FROM THE MIND OF CRITIC

JUNE 11th 2016

From the mind of critic: "If we need balance to lead a healthy and fulfilling life, how come so many of us go out of our way to be unbalanced? Are we simply trying to survive in a system greatly skewed toward the people at the top of the income scale, and away from those at the bottom? Do we simply not care about anybody but ourselves, and purposely try to better ourselves on the backs of others, calcifying the idea of vulture capitalism? We all want to better ourselves, and we all want to be included. None of us want to feel taken advantage of, but if a whole population is being is kept out of balance, so elites can hold onto what they perceive as balance, it's no wonder people are supporting any whack job who sounds like they halfway know what they're talking about. Infinite forces try to come at us whenever we allow them to, telling us how to think and live. We stay balanced by bringing ourselves joy, and doing what's right for humanity. Elites can never unbalance a balanced soul." ☺

FROM THE MIND OF CRITIC

JUNE 14th 2016

From the mind of critic: "If we're all dust in the wind, do some of us blow around more easily than others? Are some of us so devoid of substance that the wind blows us wherever it feels like it? Do some of us only look devoid to the untrained eye, because of the constant shifts in evolution? Some of us go whichever way the wind blows, while others of us will stand our ground while the wind whips our face. Our chosen action usually depends on our ambition and drive, but sometimes it's simply our environment and upbringing. While we can overcome most things, nobody can overcome everything all the time. In which case, going with the wind can be helpful just to figure ourselves out. At some point we have to pivot back to critical thought, or we'll float around forever. Some of us stand against the wind, some blow around with it. If we think critically about what's important it won't matter if we're only dust in the wind, because we know dust gives the wind its power. We the people are the grit in that dust." ☺

FROM THE MIND OF CRITIC

JUNE 15th 2016

From the mind of critic: "If life is too short to be pissed off all the time, is it okay to be pissed off some of the time? Does anger serve a purpose by spurning us to fix something we know is wrong? Does anger blind us from acting strategically, because we aren't able to put in the thought required to usher in collective and evolutionary change? It's okay to be mad. It's a normal reaction we get because we're human. All groups have dealt with wars, persecutions, prosecutions, hatred, bigotry and downright nastiness at some point during history, which causes anger to build. What makes some of these groups violent, while others stay neutral, is how they react when anger rears its ugly head. If we aren't ready to channel and focus that anger, we'll lash out violently instead of taking calm, collective and tactful action toward fixing what we were upset about in the first place. Anger can be motivation, but only when we're able to get past it, and allow the real work to begin." ☺

FROM THE MIND OF CRITIC

JUNE 16th 2016

From the mind of critic: "If light is at the end of the tunnel, do we determine the length of that tunnel? If we figure out the length, do others decipher the width, thickness and density of the tunnel? Do we design the tunnel's entire blueprints, while constantly being bombarded by advice, guidelines, suggestions, ideas, demands and recommendations? We determine our own destiny, the effort and courage required to get there comes entirely from our soul. That's not to say that life experiences and environment have no effect, they undoubtedly do, they shape our outlook and perceptions; but we're the ones who control our actions. We're the ones who decide to take things personally. We're the ones who decide what to take in, what to let go of, and what our light actually consists of. The light at the end of the tunnel and the tunnel itself, are metaphors we use when we're challenged. Once we realize the light and the tunnel only exist in our minds, we'll see that we can achieve our goals anytime, because we can access our light anytime." ☺

FROM THE MIND OF CRITIC

JUNE 17th 2016

From the mind of critic: "If we do everything today we decided not to put off till tomorrow, do we feel guilty about missing out? Do we cram as much as possible into today, because we know tomorrow might never come? Should we do what we can, feel satisfied about what we accomplished, and realize there's always more to do tomorrow and the next day, because it's part of our continuous journey? Procrastinating is a learned skill that gets imbedded over time. Once we get past procrastination, to accomplishing things sooner than later, we receive an overwhelming need to do and to act. This can make it so there's never enough hours in the day to get done we want, making us feel bad. This can cause us to procrastinate more, to keep us from getting overburdened. Just like anything in life, it's all about balancing everyday with accomplishments and joyful activities. The only time we should put things off till tomorrow, is when attempting them stresses us out to the point where we don't accomplish anything, today or tomorrow." ☺

FROM THE MIND OF CRITIC

JUNE 18th 2016

From the mind of critic: "If we use "Don't Tread On Me" as a rallying cry, do we tread on others to proclaim why our way of thinking is the best? Are our beliefs so strong that if somebody displays a different viewpoint, we think they're against everything we stand for? Do we feel a pain in the pit of our soul from being lied to and controlled for so long, that we've become cynical any good and honest people are left in the world? We all want to build better lives for ourselves and our families. We all want to live in peace and security. We all want to feel loved. We all want to be remembered and feel like we matter. We also all want the rights we're entitled to by virtue of being human. Where things get heated, is when we start feeling like others' rights, seek to de-legitimize our rights. We have the right to do, think, believe and worship however we want. What we don't have the right to do is base our rights on fake theories, false assumptions and hate. If we want people to stop treading on us, we have to stop treading on them." ☺

FROM THE MIND OF CRITIC

JUNE 21st 2016

From the mind of critic: "If we know, that if we don't learn from history we're doomed to repeat it, why do we keep repeating the same mistakes? Will we finally learn our lesson because we don't like getting hit by a 2x4 over and over again? Has so much vitriol and hateful rhetoric ingrained itself in our collective bloodstream, that it's impossible for us to learn anything new? If we're perceptive even in the slightest, we can see that we've been making the same mistakes for a long time. Whether it's war on false pretenses, religious freedoms that justify persecuting and dehumanizing others, not looking outside our own bubble, or not having 100% complete and collective equality, everywhere all the time with no exceptions, we're all sick of the same battles, lies and dead horse beatings. How do we change this paradigm? We stop hating each other, start loving each other, and start caring about more than just ourselves. History will repeat itself if we don't why it happened. We must look for the root causes of a disease to cure it. We won't find that cure, until we realize we're the disease." ☺

FROM THE MIND OF CRITIC

JUNE 22nd 2016

From the mind of critic: "If slogans and sound bites are what grab voter's attention during election time, are the voters grabbed of their own volition? Do the media only cover slogans and sound bites not issues and debates, bombarding the voters until their minds chaotically spin out of control, yearning to grab onto anything? Have the voters been purchased and persuaded for so long, that the Mount Everest of lies they've been force-fed, has caused them to be over the moon with happiness at the slightest bit of positive mediocrity? Political candidates are famous for telling voters whatever they want to hear to get elected. Whether it's the 24 your news cycle, Citizens United, or an "I want everything done yesterday" attitude, voters lose interest if explanations take too long. Whether it's "Makes America Great Again", or "Build Bridges Not Walls, we the voters need to ask why and how, and keep asking until we get an actual answer. If we complain that slogans and sound bites make up the entirety our political system, then we have to pay attention to answers which take longer than five seconds." ☺

FROM THE MIND OF CRITIC

JUNE 23rd 2016

From the mind of critic: "If we're looking for real connection, does it become easier when we realize everybody else is too, whether they admit it or not? Do we get jealous over those who are awash in real connection, not realizing it might be all for show? Do we not let jealousy overtake our reasoning skills, because we know it prevents real connection from introducing itself? Loneliness can be a roadblock to our progress. Feeling like there's nobody out there for us, prevents us from going out and experiencing new things. Maybe we've gotten to a certain age, and know we felt real connection when we were younger, but wonder if we will again. Maybe we've spent a lot of time bettering ourselves, moving forward with what we're passionate about, and learning exactly what we want. If we know what we want and what we're looking for, have we not found connection because so many other people don't know, and are freaked out that we do? I don't know the answer, but I do know hope and action keep us human and alive. If we truly want connection, we must never stop looking. Would life be worth living if we gave up?" ☺

FROM THE MIND OF CRITIC

JUNE 24th 2016

From the mind of critic: "If pride is one of the seven deadly sins, but also what we must have to move forward, how do we balance? Do we remain with our thoughts and opinions, thinking we're the most informed, not letting anything stray us from what we think is the right path? Or do we hear what everybody says, take in the good and leave the bad, and build ourselves up by taking all our experiences, and developing a way forward that's for our highest good? Do we believe enough in ourselves to make it happen? Believing in ourselves can be difficult when so many people try to tear us down. What we must remember, is the lighter that ignites the passionate inferno with our soul is not out in the world, but within us, and has been the whole time. Once we light our fire, we mustn't close ourselves from the world, because we'll immediately extinguish our fire. Our pride needs constant fuel of new experiences, and new information to be fully imagined. Our pride only becomes a deadly sin, when we let our ego overpower our critical thinking." ☺

FROM THE MIND OF CRITIC

JUNE 25th 2016

From the mind of critic: "If the sun brightly shines through our window earlier than we want, does it wash over us and prepare us for the unexpected? Do we shut our blinds, sheltering ourselves in a cocoon that keeps us from having to do anything uncomfortable? Do we open our blinds wide and let the sunlight bounce off our soul, making us believe a better world is out there if we leave our comfort zone? During the summer, the sun shines brighter, longer and earlier than it does all year. This is when we have to look within ourselves to discover what we're looking for, and what's important to us. We might be tired, we might be weary, we might even be angry to be jarred awake. The world has a funny way of telling us what we need to hear when we need to hear it, whether we're ready for it or not. Our job isn't to be upset that light is unexpected, our job is to welcome light, and use it to better humanity by reflecting light back. The morning light might be bright this time of year, but if we use it to enlighten our soul, the entire world benefits." ☺

FROM THE MIND OF CRITIC

JUNE 28th 2016

From the mind of critic: "If fog shields the coast from inland heat, does the fog also shield the people from what's really happening? Do people in power and authoritative positions, seed fog by climbing up the ladder of peasant squashing for personal gain? Do people in power become successful by forcing the fog of bread and circuses on the people, causing the people to see the fog machine and pull the plug? The fog of propaganda hangs thicker when we're stuck in the sludge of survival, believing its quicksand qualities will swallow us whole. The difference between real quicksand and metaphorical quicksand is the same as between real and fake fog. The real stuff will blind us and swallow us up no matter what. The fake stuff however, only envelopes us if we allow it to. The elite and moneyed classes use fog to keep the population scared, and willing to accept whatever is bestowed upon them. It's our job to prove fog only covers everything up, if we never ask why." ☺

FROM THE MIND OF CRITIC
JUNE 29th 2016

From the mind of critic: "If we can't kill a metaphor and can only turn it into a cliché, why do some of us insist we can kill the last terrorist? Do we actually think we can kill every single person on earth who wants to do us harm now, and in the future? Does killing the last terrorist make a great sound bite, but completely falls apart under the smallest amount of scrutiny? Wiping the slate clean and starting new has been dreamed of, since people thought the rapture would happen in their lifetime. Believing all evil people and evil acts can be deleted from our lives might work during Saturday morning cartoons, but in real life we'll never know what every person thinks. How could we kill the last terrorist if we don't know what every person thinks, which is what determines if somebody is a terrorist in first place? Killing metaphors and clichés is impossible because they're not actual things. What is possible is killing the evil attitudes that birth dark metaphors and clichés, which is a much better use of our time." ☺

FROM THE MIND OF CRITIC

JUNE 30th 2016

From the mind of critic: "If the secret to life is inner joy that we have always possessed, what do we do when somebody opens us up to possibilities that could bring us more joy than we currently possess? Does this joy introduce itself to the inner joy we already possess, and then adds to it? Does this introduction not add to our inner joy, but shows us areas of our psyche we weren't aware of, which allows us to evolve? Throughout our lives we'll come across sages, guides, lovers, friends and family that will give advice and express ideas. Part of our job is to take in the good and leave the bad, the other part is to deepen our understanding of our inner selves, further defining what we want, need and desire out of life. We need to find, then increase our inner joy. We do that by allowing ourselves to accept the world and its beauty." ☺

FROM THE MIND OF CRITIC

JULY 1st 2016

From the mind of critic: "If we believe all men are created equal, but disagree about who, what, when, how or why they were created, does it define the hypocrisy in the equality we espouse? Is the word created inserted, just to make the phrase stronger? Was it inserted by the founders not because they believed in God, but because it was written at a time when religion held a lot more sway, and the founders thought it could help people better understand equality? Mountains of hypocrisy get passed around government halls, created by the hypocrisy that's passed around civilian halls. We all want the right to live, to love, and to believe however we see fit. Once we realize everybody else does too, we'll see that we aren't really equal until everybody is equal. If equality is truly our goal, and not proselytizing how somebody else should live, we'll see that others can't be equal to us, until we're equal to them." ☺

FROM THE MIND OF CRITIC

JULY 2nd 2016

From the mind of critic: "If we all enjoy different pizza toppings, but agree we all like pizza, why do we argue over toppings when we should be happy we're eating pizza? Do we think our favorite toppings are the best, and people who like other toppings have underdeveloped and uneducated taste buds? Do we just like what we like, and realize others do too? Just how we all want pizza, we all want success, love, peace, joy and fulfillment. Once we realize all of us want these things, but believe different paths get us there, we'll see putting somebody down for their chosen path toward joy, actually destroys our path toward joy, because we're destroying our truth. With a world that can be so cold and dark, if somebody is lucky enough to find true joy, why would we ever take away the toppings which made it possible?" ☺

FROM THE MIND OF CRITIC
JULY 5th 2016

From the mind of critic: "If it's always darkest before the dawn, is it always lightest before the dark? When bright light shines from all corners, is it a sign infinite darkness is around the corner, like earthquakes, tsunamis and volcanic eruptions? Do we always think darkness is around the corner, because we think light isn't authentic? Negativity can complicate, inhibit, block and destroy any positive forward progress we've made or plan to make. If we think nothing ever works out we won't put in any effort, because what's the point if it ends up a big pile of shit anyway? If we go into situations always expecting the worst so we don't get disappointed, the light will vaporize. When we feed the light by believing positive outcomes are possible, we learn an eternal light burns within us, introducing positivity whenever we allow it to." ☺

FROM THE MIND OF CRITIC

JULY 6th 2016

From the mind of critic: "If life can be taken away at any time, what are we doing today to not take anything for granted? Are we letting our fear of death and the unknown cloud our critical thinking skills? Are we paralyzed anytime we try to do anything? Do we feel our fears and own them, using them as fuel for our journey forward? We all face different fears and worries as we trudge through our daily routine. Some of our fears are well founded in reality. When we see some poor mother balling her eyes out because her husband just got shot by the cops, while her young son tries to comfort her, but starts wailing so soul rippingly sad, his family leads him away, it can make us so fearful the cops will shoot us, we never take positive risks. Life may be short, but becomes eternal when we live how we want, and spread joy wherever we go." ☺

FROM THE MIND OF CRITIC

JULY 7th 2016

From the mind of critic: "If we're drowning in debt, how do we swim out of it if the water keeps getting deeper and deeper? Do we cinch our belt so tight, that all we purchase are the barest of essentials, negating all other qualities of life? Do we allow breathing room, so we can still feel human, even if it's a minute amount? We live in a country perfectly fine with companies charging outrageous interest, making money hand over fist from those who can least afford it. When we have to work just to pay our debt, which translates to 60% of our pay, it can be hard to see ANY light forward. The only thing we can do is keep working, and striving toward our passions. If we consciously journey while remaining kind and honest, the universe will provide what we need. At least I hope so, and sooner than later." ☺

FROM THE MIND OF CRITIC

JULY 8th 2016

From the mind of critic: "If we're angry because other people are angry, who then act out because we've acted out, where does it end? Do we keep killing each other until there's one man left standing? Do we stop killing by simply talking to each other, having a conversation about what it means to be human? When cops kill civilians unjustly, and civilians retaliate by killing cops unjustly, peaceful solutions become next to impossible to imagine. Any thinking person knows human conversation is the only solution, coincidentally, the concept is also a prime example of, "it's a lot easier said than done". Whether its race, class, religion or any issue under the sun, emotions don't change just because laws do. However, hardened emotions can soften, when we realize the hardening only happened because we allowed them to harden. Anger and hate float away when we see the other side as human. Somehow, it makes violence a much lower possibility." ☺

FROM THE MIND OF CRITIC

JULY 9th 2016

From the mind of critic: "If we've glorified violence on TV and in movies from westerns to the Mafia, and in our personal lives from vigilante groups within all facets of the political, religious, economic and racial spectrums, are we to blame when violence goes from thought to action? Have we been involved in a tit for tat since the beginning of time, simply with ever evolving weapons and words? Are we only defending what we think is right, against those who want to tear everything down? When extremes from both sides start uniting, we should be scared. The extremes both want to destroy so they can rebuild in their own image, while everyone else desires to recreate and make everything better. The less we glorify violence, the less we'll see it as the only option. The more we glorify love, peace and respect, the more solutions will emerge to save us all." ☺

FROM THE MIND OF CRITIC

JULY 13th 2016

From the mind of critic: "If we're disgusted by the state of politics, do we refuse to vote? If we're disgusted by religion, do we refuse to pray? If we're brokenhearted, do we refuse to love? When something doesn't work out how we want, sometimes we wall ourselves off so we don't get hurt. A better reaction, is taking time to get our head straight, then thinking and acting in a productive way. We owe it to our soul's journey to take whatever time we need so we're regret free. Just because somebody we don't like gets elected, or some religious nut job does something crazy, or somebody we truly love says they don't love us, doesn't mean we give up. If we do, we're letting the other side win, by letting them run our life. Which is fine, but that's our choice. Life might not always turn out how we want, but it's our choice which direction we travel, nobody else's." ☺

FROM THE MIND OF CRITIC
JULY 14th 2016

From the mind of critic: "Do the dreams that swirl around our brains, match the words that eject from our mouths? Do the words that eject from our mouths, match the beauty that emits from our hearts? Does nothing we say and feel match anything, making us ask, what's the point? Trying to figure out the world's chaos can be just that, chaotic. We want to do so many things driven by thoughts and feelings, that during implementation we sometimes act toward our own detriment, or completely opposite of what lifts us up. To balance, we must see how everything we do, affects everything else. We must see how choices for short term happiness are fleeting, and chip away at the foundation of long term happiness. The soul rejuvenating joy of dream realization and accomplishment is only possible, when we have the confidence to truly be ourselves." ☺

FROM THE MIND OF CRITIC

JULY 16th 2016

From the mind of critic: "When we argue and fight with each other about politics and religion, are we upset that the other side disagrees with us, and/or is out to destroy our side? Are we fighting simply to fight because our side has always fought the other side, even if we've forgotten why we started fighting? Do we resist fighting the other side not because we no longer disagree, but because we see who is keeping us fighting, and they don't care who wins? It seems like we've been fighting the same battles over which is the best race, the best religion, and the best political party for hundreds and thousands of years. As the majority of the world tears at each other's throats, the chess masters devise endless plans. They know if we ever saw through their bullshit, we'd stop fighting each other, unite, and rise up to fight our true enemy, them. We the people can unite. We can rise up by loving each other enough to know, only we have the power to change our world, not the elites." ☺

FROM THE MIND OF CRITIC

JULY 19th 2016

From the mind of critic: "When there's a group of people we don't know anything about, except for what we've heard from friends and the media, do we make assumptions? Have we met a few people from a specific ethnic group, been treated badly, which makes us think they're all like that? Do we know that all races, ethnicities, religions and orientations have their jerks, but the vast majority is made up of good hearted people, just like us? No group of people are monolithic, we're all unique with our own thought patterns and experiences. Racism, sexism, xenophobia and homophobia spawn from being scared of what we don't know. How do we fix that? We get to know people, more than likely we'll be pleasantly surprised. The more we see each other as human, the more human we will be." ☺

FROM THE MIND OF CRITIC

JULY 20th 2016

From the mind of critic: "If put downs get us ahead in politics, does it also work in our personal lives? If stepping on necks to succeed works in our personal lives, is it the same in our politics? If we want to make positive change in political or personal life, do we have to change both? Our personal lives and our political lives are forever intertwined by their symbiotic relationship. Sometimes politicians say some crazy and off the wall things, that are obviously racist, bigoted or meant as dog whistles. Can we honestly say we've never said those sorts of things in our personal lives? Have we ever made a despicable statement against our soul's better judgement, because we thought it would get us ahead? If we have made such statements, we are the reason our politics have gotten so out of control. If we want to make our politics more human, we have to make ourselves more human." ☺

FROM THE MIND OF CRITIC

JULY 21st 2016

From the mind of critic: "If we're tired of the same politics, the same daily routine and our same way of viewing the world, are we tired enough to try something different? Have we become so tired of ho hum results, the only thing that lifts our energy is doing something completely out of the ordinary? Are we so exhausted, that even the thought of doing or trying anything makes us want to throw in the towel and give up? Apathy and complacency can be side effects of being dog tired of world events. This low energy causes us to not pay attention, which is exactly what the people controlling things want. When we're apathetic and complacent, we won't stand up to them. Being tired is a normal human emotion, but if we truly want to save the world we must ask ourselves, are they making us tired, or is it us?" ☺

FROM THE MIND OF CRITIC

JULY 22nd 2016

From the mind of critic: If we don't celebrate our birthday, do other people not celebrate it either? Do people recognize important milestones and events in our lives, only if we recognize them? Do people help remind us to recognize and celebrate important life events, even if we've forgotten how? Now not all of us like celebrating our birthdays, and that is well within our human rights, and perfectly fine. What we must be careful of however is letting this non recognition bleed over into other parts of our lives. The world can be filled with mostly darkness or mostly light, the contrast changes depending on what we view as important. Our birthday or any day can be bright, happy, joyful and filled with gratitude, if we get out of the way of our soul's journey." ☺

FROM THE MIND OF CRITIC

JULY 28th 2016

From the mind of critic: "If we choose to celebrate our birthday by throwing a big party that nobody shows up to, is it a periscope view of our soul? Did few or no people show up, because we don't have many true friends who rise above the acquaintance or go out level? Are the few people who did show up not an indication of who is a closer friend, but of who was supposed to be there? As we get older not only will friends come and go like they always have, but who is a real friend, and who is somebody just to hang out with, becomes blindingly apparent at birthday parties. It's these personal celebrations that offer clear insights into who is celebrating because they know us and it's a fun thing to do, and who is celebrating because they actually care about us, and realize how important their presence is to us. It's always good when people show up for our birthday party, but it's even more important when friends recognize our major accomplishments. Friends make life worth living, close friends help push us forward to where we need to go." ☺

FROM THE MIND OF CRITIC

JULY 29th 2016

From the mind of critic: "If we're struggling physically, financially emotionally or spiritually and something or somebody comes along and offers a solution that might fix the problem, but goes against our principles, do we take the solution anyway? Do we utilize what they have for us, even though our mind and our soul are screaming out that it isn't right? Do we turn them down because although we may be struggling, we choose the harder, but much more fulfilling for our soul path? Life is hard sometimes, making us look wherever we can to make it easier, which is a very human thing. What we must never do is abandon our beliefs and our heart because something is easy. Life is hard and not fair, and sometimes we can struggle so much we feel like giving up, but if we do, we'll never know how truly beautiful the world can be. It's that beauty that pushes us forward, not easy solutions." ☺

FROM THE MIND OF CRITIC

JULY 30th 2016

From the mind of critic: "If we don't want to let fear drive our personal lives or our politics, why do we think demonizing the other side or those we don't agree with isn't sewing fear? Do we think fear is only being sold to us, without us selling it right back to others? Do we know that fear is being sold to us, but instead of defending ourselves by demonizing them back, we enlighten ourselves and all others by pointing out all the falsities in our demonization? It is a normal human reaction to defend ourselves when others attack us in ways we know are blatantly false, scaring others into thinking we're something we definitely aren't. If however, we scare others into supporting us by pointing out how bad the other side is, we're just as bad as them. The world is a scary enough place as it is without extra fear being proselytized for purposes of persuasion. We can let fear and hate drive us, or love and unity, there is no middle ground." ☺

FROM THE MIND OF CRITIC

AUGUST 2nd 2016

From the mind of critic: "Is there really somebody out there for each of us, or is that just something we say to make ourselves feel better when we're alone? Do we feed ourselves false hopes that we'll find love, because we're truly trying to live the old adage, fake it till you make it? Do we not believe in the concept, because we think it's just flowery language for losers? Do we honestly believe our heart and soul will sing one day, when we find that other soul that completes us? Finding somebody to love who is worthy of our love, as we are worthy of theirs, is difficult. We see all these people being happy, or at least given the opportunity to be happy, and wonder when it's going to be our time, when are we going to get our shot? Whether we believe in love for everybody or not, we all want to be loved. We might be lonely, and waiting for what seems like forever for an opportunity, but it will happen. At least I hope so." ☺

FROM THE MIND OF CRITIC

AUGUST 3rd 2016

From the mind of critic: "If one of the greatest things in life is remembering that we still have the ability to surprise ourselves, do we put a lot of undue stress on ourselves while waiting for these surprises to reveal themselves? Does this stress cause us to make whatever we have to do, seem way worse than it actually is? Does this stress get us to focus on the things we have been avoiding, which might be the keys to success we have been looking for? As we journey through life, we are going to further define what we want, and how to get it. Sometimes this involves the very things that grate on our soul, and using them to our advantage. This is when we must ask ourselves, are we going to allow uncomfortable things to stand in front of what we want. Life always comes down to choices, are we willing to be uncomfortable temporarily, so we can be joyful permanently?" ☺

FROM THE MIND OF CRITIC

AUGUST 4th 2016

From the mind of critic: "Whether earth is 5000 years old or 5 billion, does it really matter if we don't take care of it now? If man is a couple million years old, does it even matter if we don't take care of each other now? If our imagination makes us think we are as old or as young as we think, does it matter if we don't take conscious strides forward now? Many opinions about our history, politics, environment and our human nature exist. Whether we think we're an old species or a young one, whether we lived with the dinosaurs, or the earth formed for 2 billion years before we even showed up, it doesn't matter if we don't take care of each other now as well our earth, because we and it won't exist. The power of now is a real thing, and can be utilized when we stop bickering about how we screwed up before. Recognizing past issues is vital, but only if it leads to less procrastination. Our earth and our species is hurting, we must fix what's in front of us if we want the history of our age to be more evolutionary than we found it." ☺

FROM THE MIND OF CRITIC

AUGUST 5th 2016

From the mind of critic: "If doing what we've always done gives us what we've always got, how come great things happen when we persevere? Does doing the same focused thing toward a goal, eventually produce the desired results because we put in hard work? Is balancing hard work with trying new things how we stay focused on what we really want, because we're flexible and determined at the same time? There is nothing wrong with focusing on a goal, learning our process, and putting in the sustained effort to achieve it. We run into trouble when we think the hard work automatically equals success. We might be able to keep doing the same thing until we get to where we want to go. We might be able to tweak one thing, which might put us over the top because we dared to challenge ourselves by changing. Nothing in life is guaranteed whether we always do the same thing, or we always do something different. If we can balance the two, we have an infinitely better chance of success, because we allowed ourselves to be open to anything." ☺

FROM THE MIND OF CRITIC

AUGUST 6th 2016

From mind of critic: "Are the bread and circuses that anesthetize the masses, actually the first step in their enlightenment? Do the masses allow themselves to be anesthetized, because they think that having bread and having circuses is the end all be all, and don't have to progress or evolve any further, because their bare bones survival is insured? Do the masses see the wool being pulled over their eyes, and realize they must eat their bread, and be entertained by their circuses, specifically so they can expose what's actually happening? We are bombarded by messages from all angles telling us how we should do this or buy that, which attempt to guide our thinking. What we must remember is we need to be properly fed and properly entertained, so our mind is free enough to realize, that a lot more is going on than is portrayed by the corporate media. If we have to think to act, we must feed our body and mind so we can think. Bread and circuses is a trap, but they are also a jumping off point for the next revolution. As always, it is our choice whether we want to be trapped, or we want to be free." ☺

FROM THE MIND OF CRITIC
AUGUST 9th 2016

From the mind of critic: "If we know what real love is because we've felt it touch our soul, how does our soul feel when that love was so long in the past? Is it broken from never having the chance to feel anything close to real love since? Or is our soul in constant rejuvenation mode, needing constant refilling so our eyes and ears are actually open when the right opportunity comes along? Loneliness can be a powerful thing, especially when we've felt what real love feels like. We can even spend the next 15 years of our life looking to fill the void left behind. Maybe our soul has gotten close to love, but never given the chance to fully bloom. This can cause us to question if we'll ever find somebody because as we get older, the amount of singles is lower as can be our self-esteem, because we question if there is something wrong with us. This is when we have to keep up hope that we'll find somebody we have a heart connection with, because if we give up, were saying we don't deserve it. And we do deserve it, right?" ☺

FROM THE MIND OF CRITIC

AUGUST 10th 2016

From the mind of critic: "If we're passionate about an issue, and are lucky enough to grace an Olympic stage because we're amongst the world's best athletes, should we speak out? If we're given the opportunity to add voice to an issue or movement, should we take it without reservation even if the I.O.C. bans it? Are we obligated to break the law, if that law is unjust? Many political statements have been made over the years during the Olympics, whether during an event or on the medal stand. That's not to say that the Olympics are outright political, because they aren't. They're supposed to peacefully unite us by moving us beyond politics. This is where we can think we've moved beyond politics, by not thinking about them at all. When we don't think, the elites operate with impunity, because nobody questions them. If somebody stands up and says something isn't right, they get squashed. Controlling powers don't like being challenged. Are athletes trying to upset a status quo that the I.O.C. has etched in stone?" ☺

FROM THE MIND OF CRITIC

AUGUST 11th 2016

From the mind of critic: "If there aren't dumb questions, how come we don't say what's on our mind more often? How come we keep questions bottled up for so long, that when we finally vocalize them, they're filled with so much angry emotion, all we can compute is that we're the good guys, and those other guys, yeah they're bad and trying to destroy us? Have we hidden our true feelings for so long, that when we express what's wrong with the other, we're divulging to the letter what's wrong with us? Most of us, whether we're used to critically thinking about everything, or don't think about the sources of trusted information, we ask questions. The quality of what we ask depends on if we blindly follow what we hear, or point out when things don't seem quite right. The longer we hold in our true thoughts, the more vitriolic they'll be when they're released. The more we calmly and peacefully express ourselves, the less likely we'll get angry when others do the same." ☺

FROM THE MIND OF CRITIC
AUGUST 12th 2016

From the mind of critic: "If we're looking for answers to questions we haven't asked, how do we know what we're looking for? If something in the deepest part of our soul is missing, how do we find it if we can't define it? If we know we must do something but don't know what, do we randomly pick because doing something is always better than doing nothing? Trying to define indefinable ideas or events is difficult, because many things in the world don't make sense. Matters can become more difficult when we know the right questions to bring us peace of mind. Sometimes if we're lucky enough to ask the right questions, we don't always get the answers we expect, which leads to more questions. Life is basically chaos, sometimes we know the questions to ask to gain the answers we seek, and sometimes we don't. Sometimes we don't even know how to describe something with words. Do we continue our search because it isn't the answers that bring us joy, but the journey?" ☺

FROM THE MIND OF CRITIC

AUGUST 13th 2016

From the mind of critic: "If we learn the lessons of the past so we don't make the same mistakes in the future, what are we doing to ensure that brighter future in the present? Are we so worried about screwing up the future, that we spend all of our time preparing, and forget about what's right in front of our face? Do we fully understand the power of now, and how what we do in this moment encompasses the lessons of the past, affects everyone around us, and creates a future of our own choosing? Not repeating past mistakes is imperative to continuing our conscious evolution. If all we think about is being better in the future, we'll forget to be good and kind people now. If we concentrate on being those good and kind people now, our collective positive energy will rise so high, that a better future will organically sprout. Preparing for retirement or heaven can cause present day blinders. The moment we remove those blinders, is the moment we start living that better future." ☺

FROM THE MIND OF CRITIC

AUGUST 16th 2016

From the mind of critic: "Are we so scared of missing out, that to stay completely open to every possibility, that we do things we normally wouldn't, because our minds tell us it might be different this time? Do we pass over long term joy in favor of short term happiness, because we think we won't find joy till we're too old to do anything about it? Do we make ourselves happy for the moment, even though we know that moment is extremely short, and will leave us unhappier when it's over? Or do we want long term joy with every fiber of our being, because as we get older and more alone, we see it drifting further and further away as a possibility? Sometimes we can feel so depressed that we haven't found joy, we question if we ever will. This is when we have to stay open and let our light shine, no matter how long it takes. If we actually want to succeed at career and we actually want to find love, we have to stay open. Love and success will find us, hopefully." ☺

FROM THE MIND OF CRITIC

AUGUST 17th 2016

From the mind of critic: "If there's an indescribable concept, do we try to describe it anyway? If there's something we can't put words to do we try anyway, because words are how we describe things? If describing thoughts, feelings and concepts are how we make sense of the world, how do we explain chaotic events that happen on a daily basis? I heard it once said that conspiracy theories spring from us trying to make sense out of chaos. Some things don't make sense in a practical way whether it's politics, religion, the way we treat each other, or the size of our ego. Our psyche realizes we may not know how to describe something, but we know how it feels. Love is something we're all familiar with, but can never give it words that would do it justice. If something out there doesn't make sense will we attempt to explain it, or bottle up our feelings? We must ask ourselves what's more beneficial." ☺

FROM THE MIND OF CRITIC

AUGUST 18th 2016

From the mind of critic: "If we cultivate tiny seeds, and expect them to grow big and tall, do we expect perfect weather so they can? Do we believe that if we plant seeds, we can just kick back and relax because our work is done? Do we believe all we have to do is bask in the glory of our gardening prowess? Do we realize that just because we planted seeds growth isn't guaranteed, even if we accounted for millions of variables? Gardening and farming is a constant experiment just like life, where we try placing ourselves in the best position for success. The interesting part is, no matter how much we increase our chances of coming out on top, nothing is guaranteed, not even death and not even taxes. What do we do? We may not be able to guarantee success simply by putting in work, but can guarantee ourselves joy if we let gratitude wash over us for being given the chance. Nothing in life is guaranteed, except zero growth from seeds which go unplanted." ☺

FROM THE MIND OF CRITIC
AUGUST 19th 2016

From the mind of critic: "If we can't always get what we want, but try and sometimes get what we need, does that mean needs and wants have the same probability of occurrence? Do we have to put in equal amounts of effort into needs and wants to have a chance at getting them? Or do we put more effort into our needs, because they set a good foundation to allow ourselves to accept our wants? I've heard for a long time that we do what we need to do, so we can do what we want to do. We must take care of ourselves, specifically so we can take care of others. All of our needs and wants are unique, because we're all unique people. Even the ideas of needs and wants are completely subjective. What we must remember, is that all of our needs and wants might be different, but the place they spawn from is the same. We might not get what we want and need, no matter how much effort we put in. If we put in no effort at all however, we're guaranteed unfulfillment. Taking care of ourselves, is the snowball which starts the avalanche." ☺

FROM THE MIND OF CRITIC
AUGUST 20th 2016

From the mind of critic: "If we're the change we've been looking for, why don't we realize it? Why do we constantly look for satisfaction, fulfillment and joy on the outside, when it has always been inside us? Are we afraid to open up that part of ourselves, for fear of being vulnerable to all those looking to do us harm? Do we know the power our soul possesses but are weary of opening up, for fear we'll waste our time with somebody who isn't worth our time? Being the change we want to see is something we've heard for a long time. That somehow if we're authentic enough others will notice, and realize they can be authentic too. Much too often we tell ourselves that if we got this job or that house, or this person to love or that one big break, everything will change and our dreams will come true. We'll wait and wait and wait and when that outside force doesn't show, we'll get depressed and wonder if we'll ever find what we're looking for. Once we realize how much we have to be thankful for, gratitude will ooze out of our pores, and bring us people and events designed for our conscious evolution." ☺

FROM THE MIND OF CRITIC
AUGUST 23rd 2016

From the mind of critic: "If we're lucky enough to definitively and succinctly describe what we want and what we're looking for, do we wonder why so many people don't even vaguely know what they want, let alone succinctly? Are most people scrambling around just trying to survive, while spotting glimpses of what they want, but never able to latch on? Or do all of us know what we want, but are at different stages of honestly expressing ourselves, and allowing ourselves to receive what we're looking for? The world can be filled with darkness, hate and no hope, or the world can be filled with light, love and inspiration. Once we understand how our perspective guides our thoughts, which in turn creates our actions, we'll see how it's our choice what we take personally. The more negativity we inhale, the less likely we'll decipher what brings us joy. However, the more positivity we inhale, the more inner joy will naturally emanate. Inner honesty is one key to enlightenment." ☺

FROM THE MIND OF CRITIC

AUGUST 24th 2016

From the mind of critic: "If we claim honesty is the best policy, how come we keep electing politicians who don't know what that policy means? Do politicians claim honesty because it's just something to say, kind of like we do? Do we elect politicians who lie because we believe everyone lies, so we might as well elect the person who lies the least? Most of us portray ourselves as good and honest people. It's what we want the world to see, regardless of our actual character. It makes sense this feeling exponentially increases once we make it to elected office. Maybe we're scared of telling the truth because we think people can't handle it. Maybe we stretch, bend and twist the truth, because we think we can get something out of people we otherwise wouldn't. Maybe we're waiting for the truth to make sense to us, before we inform others. If we want politicians to stop lying to us, we have to stop lying to ourselves." ☺

FROM THE MIND OF CRITIC
AUGUST 25th 2016

From the mind of critic: "If we demand the law protect us when we knowingly break the law, do we believe the world owes us anything and everything? If we're illegally living in a house we don't own or haven't signed a lease for, and sue the legal property owners for turning off utilities we never paid for, do we believe we deserve for free what everybody else has to pay for? Do we simply look for a place to sleep when we're homeless, with people sometimes not liking the spots we select? We live in an age where people can illegally live on our property or break into our home, and then sue us if we evict them. There are actual laws that protect this monumentally devious behavior. There's an old saying that goes, when there are unjust laws, we're obligated to break the law. These squatters might believe they're breaking an unjust law, but so are we by telling them to leave. Civil disobedience and breaking unjust laws are required of an informed population. We must make sure we're fighting for equal rights, not for rights which nobody enjoys. We need equal, not separate." ☺

FROM THE MIND OF CRITIC

AUGUST 26th 2016

From the mind of critic: "If we're constantly asking what's the matter with Kansas, do we also ask what's the matter with ourselves? If we constantly ask what's wrong with "them" because they don't hold our values, speak our language or pay our taxes, do we ask what's wrong with us? Do we view ourselves as the gold standard, with everybody else on the planet fighting and struggling to be us, because we're perfect examples of human beings? Do we think we're the best, and all "others" want to take our stuff? When something goes wrong, we usually want to affix blame as fast as possible. We either fix problems, or explain them away. Sometimes we're to blame, but because we don't take responsibility for our actions or station in life, we blame the "other", that person with the dark skin, who speaks that weird language from that country we can't pronounce. Sometimes these "others" are from here, speak our language, but don't happen to live their lives how we think they should. If we get over our fear of self-examination, we'll see that most of our time is spent projecting onto others what we lack. Kansas has problems from time to time, but if we consciously work to fix our own problems, we'll stop projecting figments of our imagination unto others." ☺

FROM THE MIND OF CRITIC
AUGUST 27th 2016

From the mind of critic: "If two wrongs don't make a right, do two, three, four, five or six? Can we commit so many wrongs, that we know what a perfectly lived out example of what wrong looks like? Does this perfect example of what wrong is actually help us, because it shows us exactly what right looks like? Or does committing so many wrongs, make us think we'll always be wrong, so what's the point of anything? We all go through rough times as part of our collective human journey. The wrongs don't define us unless we allow them to. We can't change the bad things that have happened, but we can change our reactions to them. We have the ability to see all the wrongs we've committed, and then realize we can do the right thing. We can take all the bad we've done, and use it as a roadmap for doing better. However it's our choice, just like it's always been. We must decide on our path, we must decide on our future. If we don't, the wrongs will overtake us and take us down their path, and toward their future. Many wrongs don't make a right, unless we use them as motivation to do the right thing. We end up doing the right thing, because we can't picture ourselves doing the wrong thing anymore. We can change our direction. We just have to want to turn wheel." ☺

FROM THE MIND OF CRITIC

AUGUST 30th 2016

From the mind of critic: "If we have little pet peeves in life, do we allow them to get under our skin, making us fly off the handle? Does something completely preventable, keep happening over and over and over and over again, but nothing seems to change? Do we let this thing affect us, changing our personality from genuinely nice person into raving lunatic? Or do we take in this information that has flowed to us a million times before, but realize that the only thing in life guaranteed to change is our reactions? Many things out in the world can piss us off something fierce, whether it's politics, religion, the media, something our lover did, or something our coworker did. These forces attempt on a 24-7 365 basis to throw us off track, steering us away from the light and into the darkness. These dark forces will only get stronger the closer we get to the light, which means we have to be ready. We must allow pet peeves and darkness in for them to affect us, but it's the exact same concept with the light. We just have to ask ourselves, what will bring us more inner joy and fulfillment?" ☺

FROM THE MIND OF CRITIC

AUGUST 31st 2016

From the mind of critic: "If there's no such thing as a stupid question, how come some questions are asked not to elicit a response filled with information we actually want to know, but asked just to make the other person feel bad? Is asking a question when we already know the answer the definition of a stupid question? Are we wasting everybody's time? Or is the term stupid subjective, changing its meanings at the flip of a coin, depending on who is asking, what they know, what their intent is, and if they're running for office? We've all heard the old saying that there are no stupid questions, which goes with the assumption that stupid people don't ask questions, ignorant of how the status quo is destroying society. Maybe stupid people spit out every thought in their head without thinking about its context. Maybe smart people stay silent and observe, waiting for the full picture to emerge before they express themselves. Maybe there's no black and white answer to which is the determining factor between smarts and stupidity. Saying what we think and asking questions for needed information, is only stupid if we're doing it non-authentically." ☺

FROM THE MIND OF CRITIC

SEPTEMBER 1st 2016

From the mind of critic: "Do we believe it's always sunnier on the other side of the street, because that's what we've always been told? Do we believe the grass is always greener on the other side of the fence, because that's what we've always been told? Do we believe there is always somebody out there better than us, which prevents us from obsessing about unachievable goals? There are many things in life we think and believe, because they've always been that way. We cocoon ourselves in comfortable ruts, which can stop us from questioning why things are the way they are. If we did question, we'd realize other people think we're better than them, just like we think they're better than us. Basically it's all about perspective, the sun only appears sunnier and the grass greener, because of the angle we see it at. If we don't believe in ourselves, everything and everybody will appear better than us all the time. If however we do believe in ourselves, people will still appear better from time to time, but we'll possess the self-esteem fueled energy, to achieve what we never thought possible." ☺

FROM THE MIND OF CRITIC

SEPTEMBER 2nd 2016

From the mind of critic: "Is the reason we set goals so we constantly have something to shoot for, and have motivation to keep us moving forward? Do we set goals that are so far away, so far down the road and so much work that they're unachievable? Do we personally sabotage ourselves so we never actually achieve anything, and can stay comfortable in our imbedded cycle of poor me? Do we set our goals high because we want to achieve great things, knowing that in the pursuit of our dreams we'll probably do things we previously never thought possible? There are many things we want to do and achieve in our short time on this planet. We all must be grateful for what we currently have, while at the same time set goals born from our dreams. This gratitude is the motivation to keep us achieving, even if our goals seem far off and we've convinced ourselves we can't get there. It's important to not set ourselves up to fail when attempting impossible things. The more gratitude we hold in our heart and soul, the more we'll surprise ourselves." ☺

FROM THE MIND OF CRITIC

SEPTEMBER 3rd 2016

From the mind of critic: "If there are 2 paths we can travel in life, what's to say there isn't 3, 8, or 12 for that matter? What if there are an infinite number of paths, each with an infinite number of sub paths? Do all of these countless ways we can journey make our mind spin out of control, paralyzing our actions because we want to do everything all at once? Do we notice all of life's possibilities, and don't let them overwhelm us because we know real progress is made one step at a time? Sometimes we view society and the world, and notice all the million things that could be better, and the million solutions to make it better. Sometimes it's too much for us to handle, so we end up doing nothing. It's the same with life, and our journeys trajectory. This is when we have to slow down and pick one thing, then take the steps to make that one thing happen. We then pick the next thing, and so on. There are so many positive things we could be doing, that we're always better off doing something than doing nothing. It doesn't matter which path out of the million we choose, as long as we choose the direction. We might not always choose the right path, but if we let somebody else choose it for us, it's sure to be the wrong one." ☺

FROM THE MIND OF CRITIC
SEPTEMBER 6th 2016

From the mind of critic: "If we grew up with our parents saying, "do as I say not as I do", do we become adults who expect our actions to be excused? Do we accept zero responsibility for our actions, because we said what the right thing would have been, even though we failed to carry it out? Or do we learn that thoughts create words, words create actions, and when our parents gave us this piece of advice years ago, they were only doing it to excuse their own actions? Maybe our parents couldn't explain or excuse away, which is the entire reason they said the thing in the first place. We all had to endure events from our childhood we're not proud of, some of them we downright despise. If we want to live a productive, healthy and fulfilling life as we journey forward, we have to make the choices that'll introduce the actions that push us forward. Regardless of what happened to us, we're responsible for our actions, period. We can't just ignore bad actions we've taken, just because we said we would have liked to do something different. If we truly want to live better lives than our parents, we must not explain our actions away, but make the right choices that spawn the right actions from the very beginning." ☺

FROM THE MIND OF CRITIC

SEPTEMBER 7th 2016

From the mind of critic: "If love is really all we need, don't we need money for food, water and shelter to survive? Can money clear our obstructions, so love can be injected into the heart of the system? Or can love eliminate the need for money in the first place? Before I start I have to say food and water can be obtained for free, there's no denying that. All the people who complain that people won't work if they get free handouts, never once put themselves in the shoes of the poor. They would completely change their tune if they ever found themselves in that position. Ok, back to the chicken and the egg, does love bring money, or can money introduce love? There can be many roadblocks hindering our progress, love can break down some, and money can break down some, but neither one can do the job fully alone. We need to balance love and money to survive, just like everything else in life. The argument that money only exists because we have faith in it, is the same for love. Is having equal faith in love and money so we can survive, and live a joyful and fulfilling life, the very definition of trust the process?" ☺

FROM THE MIND OF CRITIC

SEPTEMBER 8th 2016

From the mind of critic: "If we can see clearly now because the rain is gone, does that guarantee we'll journey along the right path? If we can see all the obstacles in our way, are we guaranteed to find a way around them as we journey? If we're consciously trying to be better humans by taking care of ourselves, each other and our planet, are things guaranteed to work to our benefit? No matter how clearly we see our path or the obstacles it features, (our success, fulfillment, love, satisfaction and importance to the breadth of humankind) there are still no guarantees, no matter our consciousness level. Granted, finding our way and our impediments are only the first step, which takes conscious choice to continually move forward. Since life is always and forever a journey, and never a destination, our work is never done. We can't just sit back and relax because we think all our impediments are illuminated. We must continue making the right choices, because choice is the true determining factor in our direction. Nothing in life is guaranteed anymore, not even death and taxes. The more we're aware of our roadblocks, the much better chance we have at finding joy. Aren't those the type of odds we should be betting on?" ☺

FROM THE MIND OF CRITIC

SEPTEMBER 9th 2016

From the mind of critic: "If the secret to life is happiness, and happiness comes in different forms for different people, are we still the same basic people? If we're all unique snowflakes, aren't we all still snow? Do we divide ourselves up into groups, because it makes it easier to travel our path when the people around us are more like us? Or do we simply move forward consciously, and notice that we're much more successful when we realize people come in and out of our lives at certain times, for certain reasons? We're all struggling to find the light that will illuminate our souls with pure joy. Sometimes we think we're in it alone. Sometimes we see all the other people searching for joy, and think how can we find ours if so many people are looking for theirs? How will there be any left for us? This is when we divide up into us and them. We might think we have a better chance of finding what we're looking for, if we prevent others from finding what their looking for. Maybe this is because we think there's only a finite amount of joy out there. We must remember that the volume of joy in our world is as infinite as we allow it to be. The more we find, the more we realize our joy is linked to others. Division might serve short term happiness, but true inner joy is only found through unification." ☺

FROM THE MIND OF CRITIC
SEPTEMBER 10th 2016

From the mind of critic: "If there are so many violent people in prison, and so many non-violent people out of prison, how come so many people on the outside commit violence with impunity? Has the prison industrial complex become so rich and politically connected, that they've flipped the script, making it so the only people who go to jail, are the ones who can't fight back? Does caging all these helpless people swell the CEO'S pocketbooks? Are the people who deserve to be in jail not in jail, because their power and influence are woven so deep, that jailing them would be taking money out of CEO'S own wallets? I am all for regulated capitalism, it helps push people forward, and helps them make it on their own. Some things in life however should never be for profit, prisons being chief among them. A corrupt and morally bankrupt society is one where the few, subjugate the many for as much financial gain as they can. This isn't to say there aren't violent people in prison, because there definitely is overcrowding. Although, when poor and non-violent people are kept in prison, and rich, violent and well connected people never see the inside of prison walls, our priorities are totally backwards. How do we stop moving backwards and instead stand up and move forward? We point out hypocrisy whenever we see it. It could save our lives." ☺

FROM THE MIND OF CRITIC

SEPTEMBER 13th 2016

From the mind of critic: "If we don't know where we're going, but sure know where we've been, do we at least have a clue where we're going? If we know where we've been, and understand its historical implications, does it provide a road map? Is that road map an easily discernable and fully illuminated path forward? Or does the map's path only illuminate itself if we choose to see it? Does choice involve us using the historical implications of our past, to our advantage in the present day? We've all heard the old quote, that if we don't learn the lessons of history, we're doomed to repeat them. Once we come to a point where we actually want to learn those lessons, we start theorizing what that would look like. The theories we develop because we consciously, and courageously want to make the world a better place for all of us, is the road map we should always follow. We might not ever know 100% where we're going, but we have a much better chance of figuring it out, if we consciously better our collective world by using the lessons of the past, to learn what a better future will look like." ☺

FROM THE MIND OF CRITIC
SEPTEMBER 14th 2016

From the mind of critic: "Is life is like a hurdle race, where we're sprinting to get to the end, while simultaneously jumping over obstacles? Is life like a marathon, where we're racing to get to the end, but pace ourselves so we don't burn out early? Or is life like a decathlon, with many different events testing many different skills? One thing I've learned is that nothing in life is black and white. The moment we think it is, something comes along to prove us wrong. Kind of like when we were teenagers and thought we knew everything. Nothing in life is guaranteed except change. The ever evolving grey area where most of us live, keeps us on our toes with obstacles set in place by outside forces, and by ourselves. There are times when we understand where the finish line is, but we pace ourselves so we have a chance of reaching that end. There are other times where we're pulled in 10 different directions, and wonder which way to go, because we can't go in every direction at the same time. What we must remember is life is like an Olympic games, with ever changing and evolving events that are added or taken away on a whim. If we prepare by being open and letting our light shine, we might not be 100% guaranteed a victory, or even have any idea of what's coming. We can have guaranteed satisfaction though, if we're conscious of what's authentically in front of us." ☺

FROM THE MIND OF CRITIC
SEPTEMBER 15th 2016

From the mind of critic: "If we love letting our freak flag fly because we think it's the ultimate form of true expression, how come we roll our eyes and shake our heads when others hoist their freak flag? Do we believe the term freak is completely subjective, which causes some people's inner freak to look way different than ours? Does this in turn make us think they're detrimental to the evolution of our collective humanity? Or do we realize that when everybody flies their freak flag, it reveals the truest form of self? Do we believe when people are completely honest about who they are, the real conversation can begin? We all have facets of ourselves we keep secret, and facets we make public. The less we're scared to reveal our true nature, the more understanding, tolerant and accepting we'll be when others reveal their true nature. Revealing our own true nature and the honest thoughts that spring forth, is the key for all of us to unite around what we already know we agree on. This is simply because the untrue bullshit that fogs over reasonable discourse will no longer be a factor. Letting the world know who we truly are, doesn't guarantee we'll solve our ingrained and generational issues. It does give us the opening in the great wall we've been looking to climb through. May we all let our freak flags fly, it may save the planet." ☺

FROM THE MIND OF CRITIC
SEPTEMBER 16th 2016

From the mind of critic: "Do we expect technology to fix all our environmental problems, because we choose to keep polluting? Do we expect technology to fix all our health issues, because we choose to eat junk food, and to live an unhealthy lifestyle? If we expect technology to do everything for us, are we trying to be as lazy as possible? In the last 50 years there have been many technological advances. They have extended our life span, and made our day to day life easier by freeing up time for more fulfilling ventures. Where we go wrong is when we think we don't have to advance our thinking, ourselves, our society and our world along with the technology which outpaces itself every 2 years. It's not that ever increasingly advanced technology isn't wanted, because it is. If we ate better foods, didn't spill deadly toxins into the soil or release them into the air, and didn't tear each other down, we wouldn't be in such urgent need of technology. As technology grows, our consciousness must grow along with it. We don't want to be left holding the proverbial bag when technology implodes, and we have to reconstruct our humanity. We must choose to make a better future now, not rely on technology to do it down the road." ☺

FROM THE MIND OF CRITIC

SEPTEMBER 17th 2016

From the mind of critic: "When did we become a country which applauds and touts people simply for not being racists, bigots or homophobes? When did we start praising those who treat others with respect, when it's something they should have been doing all along? When did we come to the realization that the world is so messed up, that we get elated at the most mediocre bit of light, truth and consciousness? We have a lot of issues in our society, there's no denying that fact. We've grown comfortable with evil and the darkness taking away our decency toward each other. Maybe we do nothing because we believe it is what it is. Maybe we get past celebrating mediocrity, by not putting somebody on a pedestal for doing something they should be doing anyway. Maybe we can stop treating each other as stepping stones or commodities, but as part of the same human family. The more we celebrate somebody for not being a jerk, or for finally admitting they were a jerk, the less we'll progress forward. We want to progress forward, right?" ☺

FROM THE MIND OF CRITIC
SEPTEMBER 20th 2016

From the mind of critic: "If this land is your land, but it's also my land, why don't we just say it's our land? Are we afraid we'll cede our supremacy for the other side's inferiority, or afraid they'll cede their inferiority for our supremacy? Are we afraid of the idea of our land, because we always thought property would exist, but not rights? The argument could be made that Woody Guthrie and John Lennon expressed the same idea, that the ground of this earth belongs to all of us, specifically because we're human, and all on this earth. This land is made for all of us, not just a few of us. This land wasn't made for just the rich and powerful, or a group that speaks, acts and worships the same because they display the same amount of melanin. Where we go wrong is when we believe in "our" land so harshly, that we kill all dissidents, or cordon them off in refugee camps or prisons if we can't kick them out. Many, many wars have been fought, many are being fought now, and unfortunately more will definitely be fought in the future. While nobody wants to live in a war zone, we'll all be living in war zones if we keep hardening our stances of my and yours, and us and them. Peace is only achieved through unification, not separation." ☺

FROM THE MIND OF CRITIC

SEPTEMBER 21st 2016

From the mind of critic: "When did union become a bad word in this country, was it the same time that liberal became a bad word? Was it because we got so hung up on the little things that we forgot about the bigger picture? Or were we so focused on the bigger picture that we forgot it's the little things that make life worth living? Do we realize that it's those little things that make the bigger picture what it is? We enjoy the fruits of our labor, good and bad. This point in our history didn't fall out of the sky. This has been building for a very long time. All those laws and rules that made union and liberal a good word, have been so chipped away, that its turned them bad. Maybe we realize we can't make the radical and drastic changes we want all at once, so we put in the hard work, and do all the mundane tasks, so our opponent doesn't see their entire world changing around them. Without unions and liberals we wouldn't have half the things we do, just like without language we wouldn't be able to state what we really feel. Without choice, we are completely helpless. Isn't choice what we're giving up when we enjoy something we know has bettered our lives, yet still portray it as evil and destructive?" ☺

FROM THE MIND OF CRITIC

SEPTEMBER 22nd 2016

From the mind of critic: "If there are an infinite number of perspectives on an infinite number of subjects, how do we know which one is the right one? Is there a way to correlate, quantify and explain an algorithm in such a way, that all humans understand in black and white what's the best way to think? Or is it all chaos, and the more we believe that one perspective is better than another, the more chaotic we make situations? We all know the old adage, "the more we think we know, the more we don't know". The more we think we have it figured out, the more it proves we have much further to go. None of our perspectives are better than anybody else's, however the more we voice our perspective, the more others will display theirs. The more of us that get used to displaying our opinions while hearing others', the more we'll see that the breadth of the world's chaos is describable. Perspectives are like assholes or dreams, we all have them. How we choose to use them, might not ever fully define the chaos, but will govern the future of our planet." ☺

FROM THE MIND OF CRITIC

SEPTEMBER 23rd 2016

From the mind of critic: "If we're informed consumers when shopping, what about when trying to find an avenue to make positive change? Do we hunt and search for ways to make big statements? Do we spend a lot of time and effort setting it up, just to go home afterward? Or do we search for ways to help humanity long term? Do we do this so seven generations down the line they'll look back, and say they're glad something actually fixed the problem, and didn't just make a statement? We could be doing many things on a daily basis to make our lives better. If we spend six months looking for a car, making sure we check all the specs, we could use the same tenacity when searching for methods for making long lasting positive change. If we use coupons, wait for half price sales or buy one get free, we try to make the most out of what we have, so it has long lasting effects. Once we realize we have the talent and the ability in our toolkit, we'll see we can make all our collective dreams come true. We can't only be informed consumers, but must be informed humans as well. We must choose the right method, and then go for it. We can find the right solutions. We just have to take some time to flush them out." ☺

FROM THE MIND OF CRITIC

SEPTEMBER 27th 2016

From the mind of critic: "If presidential debates are supposed to help us determine who should be president, how are we supposed to learn anything if they repeat the same thing they've been saying for months? Will their overused terms, statements and focused grouped phrases sound new to us, if we haven't been paying attention before the debates? Is that the only way a rationally thinking person could think these actually are debates? Some of us don't watch sports until the playoffs, because we believe the games are better near the end of the season. Maybe some of us believe the debates are when things get really good. Maybe we aren't watching to gather information, but as pure entertainment. Maybe debates are the ultimate reality show, where people always do crazy and unexpected things. Maybe this explains exactly what's wrong with our system. When the extremes of one side are so scared of the extremes from the other, that each sides best bet is to run Biff Tannon against a pre-corronated queen, the next logical step is for the extremes to unite because they're extreme, against everybody else who is "normal". This is when things will get really bad. Debates will only be real, when candidates are fact-checked by the moderator as they speak. That is unless we want our system to devolve into a Jersey Shore marathon, and nobody wants that." ☺

FROM THE MIND OF CRITIC

SEPTEMBER 28th 2016

From the mind of critic: "If seeking truth requires us to acknowledge hypocrisy, does it also require us to ask questions, live authentically, and love like our lives and our world depended on it? Does it require us to let go of all our pre and mis-conceptions? Does it require us to drop all labels? Clear all roadblocks? Should we quit stepping on others to succeed? Should we be obligated to help others in their journey, as so many have helped us? The term seeking truth is extremely subjective, being that there's infinite ways we could seek or not seek it. What's the same however, is no matter what method we use to find whatever form our truth comes in, we all must be open and willing to accept it, even if it's something we don't want to hear. Part of being open, is letting our light shine. Part of letting our light shine, is pointing out when things aren't right, standing up for what we believe in, and being the change we want to see. Seeking truth starts with us being truthful to and about ourselves, specifically so we can be truthful to and about others. We must let truth do what it was designed to do, unite us." ☺

FROM THE MIND OF CRITIC
SEPTEMBER 29th 2016

From the mind of critic: "If closed minds usually come with open mouths, do closed minds ever come with closed mouths? Do open minds ever come with open mouths? Or does the mere concept of an open mind require a closed mouth, because the only real way to be open to everything is by not continuously spewing commentary? There are infinite variables in infinite equations that explain an infinite amount of situations. What we can count on, is that nothing is black and white. Whether somebody has a closed or open mind, it offers no indication of a closed or open mouth. People with open minds should speak more, and people with closed minds should speak less. Loving and taking care of each other and ourselves, ensures that we never close our mind to problems of the world, and always open our minds to all the good in the world. We all must talk and ask questions, but also listen and comprehend. The more we get used to talking to each other like human beings, the more our closed minds will naturally open." ☺

FROM THE MIND OF CRITIC

SEPTEMBER 30th 2016

From the mind of critic: "If we hated waking up early for school, but never for Saturday morning cartoons at 6am, did it make us do only what we want, and never what we need? Do we wake up every day and only do what we want because it's instant gratification, instead of doing what we need so we survive in the long run? Or do we understand the balance we must live with needs and wants, so that we're joyful and fulfilled to the point where we smile, because we know we're walking the right path? My mom has told me for years that we have to do what we need to do, specifically so we can do what we want to do. This concept lays a strong foundation to start building our life. Once we have this strong start, we'll feel like we earned the good things in life. We'll feel confident about doing what we want, because we've put in the work. If we only pay attention to our needs and never our wants, we will live joyless, and lonely lives. We'll strive to get a little further ahead of our neighbor, who we'll get increasingly jealous at randomly. We can find balance, we can succeed, and we can achieve our dreams. We just have to afford ourselves the opportunity." ☺

FROM THE MIND OF CRITIC

OCTOBER 1st 2016

From the mind of critic: "If doing what we've always done gets us what we've always got, does doing something different guarantee different results? If we change our routine, will the outcome be different by virtue of different variables going into the equation? Or is it all basically chaos, and the best we can hope for is changing things up? Doing the same thing over and over while expecting different results, is the definition of insanity; which might help explain our world and current governments. Some our greatest inventors, movement leaders, activists, thinkers and heroes however were only successful because they never gave up. Sure, people told them they were crazy for doing something over and over, expecting it to eventually work out. Our greatest historical figures would never have succeeded if they heeded the advice. They felt in their hearts, minds and the deepest part of their souls they were doing the right thing. They felt eventually their dreams would become reality, because the energy driving them was bigger than themselves. Quantifying that energy, whether somebody actually has it, or is just on drugs or dense, is impossible to know. The best we can do, is what our heart and soul tells us to do, and then not stop. We might not ever have guaranteed success, but we can have guaranteed fulfillment." ☺

FROM THE MIND OF CRITIC

OCTOBER 4th 2016

From the mind of critic: "If it's the darkest right before the dawn, is it the lightest right before the dark? Is there a difference between saying, it gets really bad before it gets really good, and saying it gets really good before it gets really bad? Or is it just something we tell ourselves because we're experts at self-sabotage, thinking nothing good will happen unless something terrible happens afterwards? We've all had times in our life, when it seems like nothing can work out; when we get let down time after time after time, sometimes because of our own doing, and sometimes not. This can make it extremely hard to think about not only positive things to come, but also gratitude for everything we have now. Whether we fake it till we make it, or simply put in extra effort, it'll seem strange at first because it's something out of the ordinary. The more we do it, the more we'll get used to it as just something we do. Whether it's dark before the dawn or dawn before the dark, light only appears if we allow it to." ☺

FROM THE MIND OF CRITIC
OCTOBER 5th 2016

From the mind of critic: "If we say "when it rains it pours" when something goes wrong and gets progressively worse, do we also say "when it rains it pours" when something goes well and gets progressively better? Are we so used to expecting the worst, that it feels weird to even allow ourselves to take pride when things are becoming progressively better? Or has life gotten so fake and phony because of its distance from nature, that we can't tell when something is authentically going good or authentically bad, so we assume it's bad because that's what we've always done? There's a lot of darkness in life that can overshadow light. It can be easy for us to fall into the comfortable rut of expecting the worst, so we know what's ahead. This can make us so cynical and skeptical that whenever we see a small glimpse of light, we figure it's a wolf in sheep's clothing. We must remember life is full of schedules, routines and ho-hum everyday activities. The more we normalize bad events, the more ingrained they'll get as something that just happens. When we start normalizing good and enlightening events, the more they will get ingrained in us. We are creatures of habit. We assume what's happening, will continue to happen, until we can move onto more important matters. Won't we get much further along in life if we say "when it rains it pours" when something good happens, instead of just grabbing a raincoat?" ☺

FROM THE MIND OF CRITIC

OCTOBER 6th 2016

From the mind of critic: "If things haven't worked out in a long time, despite all the effort, wanting and positive thought put in, is there a way to stop self-sabotage from taking over our critical thinking skills? Will we decide that negativity has always felt bad, but since we expect it to happen and rarely get let down, does it actually makes us feel comfortable? Do we realize negativity moves us backwards, and although positivity can be hard work, it does move us forward? Sometimes when we want something so badly it oozes out of our pores, and scares off people that may help us get what we want. Whether it's success in our chosen career, or finding love, how do we stop looking for something we really want? If what we want shows up when we stop looking, how on earth do we stop looking for something we truly want? Is it just something people say that have already found some form of what we're looking for? If I really want a love that makes my soul sing, that makes me high just being around her, and somebody tells me I can only find it if I stop looking, how exactly does that work? Has that advice giver ever thought about how that would play out in real life? I might be lonely and looking for that special love like a lot of us might be. Will we ever find it, who knows? I know things might not have worked before, but if we ever want things to work out in the future, we must leave ourselves open to the possibility that they will work out." ☺

FROM THE MIND OF CRITIC
OCTOBER 7th 2016

From the mind of critic: "If the government is drowning in a pool of debt, is it because we're personally drowning in a pool of debt? If we're drowning, is it because wealth is being condensed in fewer and fewer hands, making it so the government can only function if it accepts more debt, because it takes in much less revenue? Are we making an honest living honestly, while pursuing our passions in the little spare time we contain? Does this make our debt worse because we're trying to make our soul shine, while so many others in our society aren't? Whether its education loan debt, credit card debt or any other debt we've incurred to survive, it's not sustainable. We need to pull in more money to pay that debt. When we can't earn more money in an honest or legal way, our debt gets worse, just like the governments. The reason the government is in so much debt however, is because many people escape their debt by either tax havens, loopholes or other immoral means. Our country has plenty of money, it's just concentrated. How do we change our trajectory? Once we realize that honesty, passion and kindness are the only true measure of success, we'll see that to change society, we must change ourselves. One person can change the world, by starting a tidal wave of change.

To end our indentured servitude, we must accept the reason it happened, even if we don't want to hear the answer. To change honestly change the world, we must honestly change ourselves." ☺

FROM THE MIND OF CRITIC
OCTOBER 8th 2016

From the mind of critic: "If the great feeling we have when we end our week on Friday, is the exact opposite of the bad feeling we have when we start our week on Monday, do we ever wonder why? Is it because we have so little spare time, or time to ourselves that we become miserable when the last bit of it drips away? Do we become unhappy on Monday, because we failed to spend the little time we had to uplift our soul, dashing the hopes we may have had on Friday afternoon? Whether we have a case of the Mondays, or are just nervous about starting a new week, it's imperative we spend more "us" time feeding our passions, our souls and filling our tool kit with ways to handle and react to all of life's random issues. These moments will become normal as we work them into our routine. They are the foundation for not only a better life, but a better world. The more of us that spend this time and don't kill it, not only will our Mondays be less miserable, but so will our lives in general. Life is short as all of us could attest to, the best thing we can do for the collective evolution of the planet, is never waste or kill time, but enjoy time, and spend it making our soul shine. If we do, we'll never have a case of the Mondays again, because every day will seem like Friday with all the opportunities which abound." ☺

FROM THE MIND OF CRITIC
OCTOBER 11th 2016

From the mind of critic: "If somebody running for political office utters outrageous, sexist, racist and dictatorial phrases, why do we get surprised when they've been saying these things for years? Did we honestly think they would stop when they got on a national stage? Do we get shocked at these increasingly outrageous comments, because we didn't think they could get any worse? Or do we see the outcropping of what has been simmering for years, and see it as a natural evolution of events? We've gotten desensitized over the years by generations of an "if it bleeds it leads mentality". Maybe it's a natural evolution of regular people not taking care of each other, but tearing each other down by creating three classes of people, the spewers, the people who get shocked, and the people who tune out. We're all at different levels in our journey, which could explain our reactions, and if we have open or closed minds and mouths. Once we realize that how we treat each other not only reflects what kind of person we are, but also the kind of person others want us to be, we'll see that politicians, business leaders and people trying to reach high office, only say crazy things to the public, because they hear the public saying crazy things to each other. Not only do we have to be the change we want to see, but we must act on it like no other time in history." ☺

FROM THE MIND OF CRITIC

OCTOBER 12th 2016

From the mind of critic: "If the way to a person's heart is through their stomach, is the way to their mind through their heart? Is the way to a person's soul through their mind? Is the way to evolution and conscious revolution through our collective souls? Or is it waiting for the right person or event to come along, where the change will be made outside of our control? Is this because we believe we can never make change ourselves? Food is an important part of our society. It's the fuel that powers our mind. This not only makes the conscious evolution and revolution of humanity and the spirit possible, but shows us all how we're not that different from each other. Food is also a great example of how everything is interconnected. The best food can only be grown with good weather, soil, air and water, basically a healthy environment. Good food can only be manufactured with hard working, happy and productive employees. This means strong labor laws, pay and worker morale are imperative. Food can also only be healthy with strong safety regulations and rules against fraud. This means a government that is accountable to the people. To make conscious thought the standard, and to make the evolution of our revolution inevitable, we must connect to each other's souls through our minds and hearts. How we connect to somebody's heart is through their stomach.

The way to create the good fuel for that stomach which gets the ball rolling, is taking care of our environment, having strong labor laws and unions, as well as an accountable government. If that's what all of us dream of anyway, are we finally ready to personally put in the effort to make that a reality?" ☺

FROM THE MIND OF CRITIC
OCTOBER 13th 2016

From the mind of critic: "If the fate of our conscious evolution and humanity depends on our choices, how do we make choices to ensure our collective forward trajectory? If the fate of our personal well-being, love, life and career success depends on our choices, how do we make choices to ensure our personal forward trajectory? Is the personal and collective journey antithetical to each other, where one side only finds success if the other fails? Or is the personal and collective journey a symbiotic relationship, where each side only find success if they build each other up? Do unto others as we would have them do unto us, is an old saying we've heard for a long time. Have we ever spent time to examine what that actually means, and how it plays out in real life? We're all part of the collective, as well as the personal. If we don't take care of ourselves we'll be bitter and grumpy when the collective asks us to take care of it. We might feel like they're stealing our time, preventing us from taking care of ourselves. On the flip side if we never take care of the collective and only ourselves, our success and happiness will be fleeting because we don't have anybody to share joy with, because we feel like we're better than everyone else. What about choice? It comes in whenever we take action, whatever direction we decide to travel in. We must decipher which path is best for us, and what is best for the collective. That balance, is one of the keys to life.

Life might be chaotic, dark, and seem like it'll never work out. However, deciding to take care of ourselves, specifically so we can take care of others, makes our journey into the dark unknown much less scary. It creates light at the end of the tunnel." ☺

FROM THE MIND OF CRITIC
OCTOBER 14th 2016

From the mind of critic: "If our political system is based on the idea of whoever has the most money makes the rules, do those same rules apply to our personal lives? Is it any wonder elected officials with the most influence are the ones, who have the richest people in their pockets? Do the vast majority of the super-rich believe they can live their lives with impunity? Is this because we think people with alot of money are successful? Do we think they're above all the little people, and don't have to be governed by the same rules and justice system? Do we know the evolutionary setbacks this way of thinking causes and are fighting back against it? Is it such a long, hard and slow march to progress, that any positive change is extremely hard to see? If the people with all the gold make the rules, it's because we've allowed that to happen. Some of us think if somebody has money and influence, they must know more about what's wrong and how to fix it. We might see this and relinquish our control. Once we realize that taking back control means standing up and never sitting again, our generationally ingrained problems float away, and politicians beholden to the super rich will cease to exist. If we stop automatically revering the super-rich simply for being super rich, we'll stop corrupt politicians from being created. To fix our political system we must fix our personal system. To do that, we must cherish what's actually real, not what we think is real." ☺

FROM THE MIND OF CRITIC

OCTOBER 17th 2016

From the mind of critic: "If life isn't always as it seems, and things are closer than they appear, how do we know what's real? Are we awash in a sea of chaos, where it doesn't matter where we go or what we do, because we think even if our goals and dreams have come true, there is no 100%, guaranteed and fool-proof way to prove their authenticity? Is nothing in life black and white, no matter how much we want it to be? Do we get glimpses of good moments, bad moments and everything in between? Do these glimpses help us decide what's real, what's fake, what we should hold onto, and what we should let release? Life, and trying to create a joyful routine that can be adjusted when positive opportunities arise, are the most challenging decisions we can make, but also the most rewarding. If people appear one way, they could be the opposite. Their facial expressions could make them look happy, but they might actually be depressed. Just as there is multiple sides to every situation, there are multiple choices we face with every moment of every day. They could either be to our benefit, or our detriment. If we don't choose because we don't want to or don't know how, we still have made a choice. Everything in life is fake but real at the same time, depending on our perception. When we choose to build ourselves up instead of tear ourselves down, we'll ensure our souls joy as we journey into the unknown of endless choices and perceptions." ☺

FROM THE MIND OF CRITIC

OCTOBER 18th 2016

From the mind of critic: "If the secret to a fulfilling life is finding purpose, will we automatically know it when it arises? Will it smack us in the head like a 2×4, describing in the plainest, black and white language it can that it's the answer to our dreams? Or is it something that'll sneak in like a whispering wind, where we have to be 100% completely open and conscious to even get a glimpse, let alone to take advantage? We should all breathe a little easier knowing all of us are searching for purpose, all discovering, deciphering and decoding as we journey. We aren't alone. We're just at different points in our similarly unique and unknown expeditions. Great things might happen all at once, and good things might take time, but if we aren't open to the universe, and aren't willing to put in the effort when more work is required, we won't be able to get, let alone accept good or great things. If we can't accept good or great things, we certainly won't be ready to accept our purpose when it comes along, whether it's obvious, or takes work to fully define. Nobody can tell us what our purpose is. It touches the deepest part of our soul. There are many secrets to life, chief among them is feeling like we count, and feeling like we matter. Finding purpose can be easy, or it can be the hardest thing we've ever done. The reward however is guaranteed to provide us positive energy beyond our wildest dreams." ☺

FROM THE MIND OF CRITIC
OCTOBER 19th 2016

From the mind of critic: "If we constantly rail on the other side for not talking about the issues, say we want somebody who'll bring positive change by instituting ideas that'll benefit us all, but then turn around and vote for somebody because they tug at our heart strings, completely forgetting what we said we cared about, is it any wonder we get two candidates nobody likes? Are we trying to look good in front of our friends by telling them anything they want to hear, only to do and say whatever we want anyway when they're not around? Do we have sinister thoughts about trying to take advantage of everybody and everything, because although we say we care about others, we really only care about ourselves? Have we never paid attention or cared about what's going on in the world, but now that everybody is going nuts, we figure we should too? Politics always has been and always will be a reflection of our society. If politicians or those seeking office are two-faced, are constantly flip-flopping or hold differing opinions depending on who they're around, is it any wonder that we let it be known that there are subjects we don't discuss? Maybe we're afraid to tell people what we really think, because we're afraid we'll be judged, and can't stand somebody not liking us. Is it any wonder we're willing to say anything to anybody?

If we ever hope to not have an election where we have to decide between douches and turds that make our skin crawl, we must be authentic, speak from the heart, and not care if somebody doesn't like us. When we free our minds, we free our souls. Free souls are the only place politicians should come from." ☺

FROM THE MIND OF CRITIC

OCTOBER 22nd 2016

From the mind of critic: "If we've reached a point where we know what we want and what we don't want, does it make it harder to get what we want because we're more picky? Are the end results we dream of harder to achieve, because our choices are clear as to what's to our benefit, and what's to our detriment? Is it harder to achieve our dreams, because although we know what we want, so many others out there (who might be amongst those who helped us achieve what we want) don't know what they want themselves, and therefore are unwilling or unable to help anybody else? Is it a combination of the two? Spending time to figure out, find, discover, explore and experience what we want, doesn't mean it'll fall in our lap. Maybe we're being tested by having adversity thrown in our face. Maybe the adversity is self-inflicted, because although we know what we want, we haven't found it yet. Are all these people who seemingly have found what they want, just putting up a front because they aren't happy? Maybe they haven't found what they truly want and feel they have to go through the motions, because they think that's what society wants. We might not have control over what we want, but figuring out what we want is the first step in achieving it. Will we ever get what we want or deserve, who knows. Will we figure out what we want if we stay open, conscious and kind so we can take advantage of opportunities, absolutely." ☺

FROM THE MIND OF CRITIC
OCTOBER 24th 2016

From the mind of critic: "Have we finally reached a point in society where everything is breaking down, where common decency, common sense and logic have flown out the window, in favor of hate, ignorance, and unfounded arguments? Have the extremes gotten so extreme, that all the people who aren't polar opposites, are sandwiched in the middle, and seen as the extremists because they aren't extreme? Or is everything so raw right now because of major change, that some of us retreat to our ignorance to protect ourselves? Do some of us proselytize that our way is the best, while the rest of us using opportunities as a learning experience, so the change can be positive, conscious and benefit everybody? Whatever side we're on, or whatever we believe or don't believe in, we could all agree major change is afoot. Our society is changing as it does every generation. We're just feeling it more now. We all have different coping skills, and deal with change differently. Once we realize none of us can do better until all of us do better, we'll see that lifting each other up instead of tearing each other down, is the only way to build ourselves up. Some of us fear change, and some of us welcome it. The more rights, freedoms and kindness we show others, the more we'll realize they're more like us. The more we realize that, we'll see that when we tear somebody else down, we're really tearing ourselves down.

We have a chance to usher in the next positive and conscious step in our collective evolution. No matter what, that evolutionary step will happen. The only question is will it happen in spite of us, or because of us?" ☺

FROM THE MIND OF CRITIC
OCTOBER 25th 2016

From the mind of critic: "If we're lucky enough to have found our passion, and have discovered that this passion involves creating something which provides healthy escape filled with conscious thought, social justice and self-love rippling into collective love, do we shy away from using that same method of escape when somebody else creates it? Do we believe that being present here and now is what allowed us to find our passion in the first place? Are we afraid we'll lose all the ground we gained in our conscious evolution, because we're giving into the very thing that drives us away from the authentic? Are we ultra-conscious of our personal journey of discovery, and want to be present for every beautiful moment of it? I've been asking myself these questions for a while. Do I shy away from reading books, because I see them as an escape that pulls me away from the present, which is what helped me realize my passion for writing books in the first place, and gives me the positive energy to do so? It's all part of a positive-negative balance we all must achieve. It's the realization of who we are, who we'd like to evolve into, and how to make that happen. Are we ready to put our full energy into our passion, releasing the full amount of effort required to succeed? Escape can be healthy, as long we're not using it to escape what brings us pure joy, but using it to refresh our mind, body and soul, so we're ready to give our passion the full effort it deserves.

Once we realize that passion and escape aren't antithetical to each other but symbiotic, we'll see how much farther ahead we can get if we allow our soul to feel joy." ☺

FROM THE MIND OF CRITIC
OCTOBER 26th 2016

From the mind of critic: "If searching for truth reaches to the very essence of who we are, does the fact that we may never fully find it, (because truth is subjective and can change from person to person) make us question our very existence? Does authentically, passionately and consciously looking for what's real set us up for failure, because truth changes depending on our perception? Or is it all just one big leap into the unknown, where the answers can change because they're subjective? Since the unknown by definition is unknown, do we keep moving forward because we realize we've always had the ability to surprise ourselves? When the world looks phony because everybody is getting away from what's real, it's not surprising we search for truth whether we want to admit it or not. I'm not talking just about voters during an election season. All of our truth searches might be for different things, but I'll bet none of us can fully define what we're searching for. That fact, that we're all consciously or unconsciously searching for something that we can't fully define, should make us all realize what drives us is basically the same. We'll see that the small and insignificant things which keep us apart, skews the truth. The object of our unique but similar searches for truth, have been right in front of us the whole time." ☺

FROM THE MIND OF CRITIC
OCTOBER 27th 2016

From the mind of critic: "If many of us in the last few weeks, months and years have asked how politicians could possibly say the most biased, outrageous, offensive and vial things, have we asked ourselves the same questions? Do we believe the system has been so skewed from the beginning, that office holders can say anything they want, Do we believe as long as they keep throwing crumbs, the people will put up with it? Do we think that this acting out is so far from a normal person's actions, that it leads us to believe these politicians aren't human? Or do we see politicians acting out as a natural outcropping of the way we've been treating each other for generations, which makes politicians not only human, but it makes them us? We're all familiar with the concept of not talking about religion and politics with friends and family. Maybe we've grown so used to not talking about them, that we don't realize others have too. With all the voluntary heads sticking themselves in the sand, some are actively and continuously scheming how to control us. We've been doing this so long that we resort to personal attacks. Maybe we've blinded ourselves to what we're actually saying, because we think it's conversation, when it's actually the complete opposite. To stop politicians from saying vial things, we need to stop saying vial things. To do that, we need to be open and honest about how we feel on every subject.

What we think are things we should never talk about, might be what saves us. The unknown is only scary because we see it that way. If we change our perceptions, we can change the world." ☺

FROM THE MIND OF CRITIC

OCTOBER 28th 2016

From the mind of critic: "If manifesting what we want is how we get it, does obsessing about it drive it away? Is there a way to balance manifestation and not overthinking, therefore creating the happy medium we want? Or are we kidding ourselves when we think this balance can be achieved, because it's not possible to think about something, and not think about something at the same time? Figuring, deciding, choosing and deciphering what we want can be a challenge. Once we figure it out, the next step is how we bring it in to our lives. Maybe it's a universal challenge that all of us go through. Whether its love, success in career, or whatever we authentically believe will improve our lives, we've been told to either manifest what we want, or not think about something. Maybe this is like getting advice from too many people, so we end up doing nothing. Maybe it's like the natural push and pull of life, we must discover how to be fulfilled and successful. Maybe we need to take the good from both sides to create our own way of being, so we don't blindly follow anybody or anything. Whether manifesting or letting go gets us what we want faster, we'll never know. However, if we stay open and let our light shine, we will receive everything we're supposed to." ☺

FROM THE MIND OF CRITIC
OCTOBER 29th 2016

From the mind of critic: "If it's inevitable that we turn out like each of our parents, how do we ensure that we keep the good and let go of the bad? Do we have control over what characteristics create our personality and decision making abilities? Or do we just float through life with no control over what may or may not have happened when we were younger, and are doomed to repeat our parents' bad deeds and choices because it's in our genes? Some of us had terrible childhoods with terrible parents. Some of us had great childhoods with great parents. Some of us had a mixture of the two. What we all know is true, is that if we don't learn from the past, we're doomed to repeat it. If bad things were perpetuated on us, we will perpetuate bad things onto others. If however we perpetuate the good, it's not bad that it gets repeated. How do we ensure that nothing is automatic? Once we realize that we always have choice concerning our actions and reactions, and black and white thinking doesn't give an honest portrayal of the good or the bad, we'll see we aren't doomed to repeat anything unless we allow the rerun. Nothing in life is inevitable, or guaranteed, not even death and taxes. We always have choice. We can choose what to take in, and what to discard. We can choose what's to our benefit, and what's to our detriment.

Each of our parents have good and bad qualities. It is and always has been up to us to decide and decipher what's what. If we don't choose, somebody else will. The more we choose our own destiny, the more it will help further our collective and conscious evolution." ☺

FROM THE MIND OF CRITIC
NOVEMBER 1st 2016

From the mind of critic: "If often times it happens that we live our lives in chains, why do we never know we have the key? Are we so comfortable with the chains that surround us, that although we know they're detrimental and specifically responsible for our downfall, they're familiar, and so we go with what's comfortable but conforming, instead of what's unknown and freeing? Will fear of the unknown flatten us the moment we try to better ourselves? Are we uncomfortable with our situation, causing endless possibilities to spin us out of control? Has the key gotten lost in the shuffle? Many things in life can block our physical, emotional, spiritual, financial and evolutionary progress. Sometimes they come from the outside, but the majority of the time they're self-inflicted. Why aren't there more of us who build others up? Why we don't take time to build ourselves up? Maybe our self-deprecation has ballooned so large, that we've convinced ourselves we don't deserve happiness. If we saw this self-inflicted reverse psychology for what it is, we'd grab that crusty old key, jam it in that rusted over lock, and bust through the chains that have been holding us back. Whether we're awakening to the fact that we've always had the key, or think about it every second of every day, we, and only we have the power to unlock our chains. We can unlock them, but we have to want to, and we want to, right?" ☺

FROM THE MIND OF CRITIC
NOVEMBER 2nd 2016

From the mind of critic: "With the grand canyon size differences between the candidates we've been given to choose from, how did we become so complacent, apathetic, and just plain indifferent about either one? Have we evolved past picking between the lesser of two evils, to not picking who we want, but picking the person we feel has the best chance of beating the person we don't want? Have we devolved so much that we don't believe what anybody says, and vote based on emotion? Thinking about what we want, how it melds together with how others' want to help the planet consciously evolve, is how we got here. Or should I say, not doing that has brought us here. Maybe we've given up on things presently improving, so we become nostalgic about the past. Have we become so lazy, that we only talk about the old days, and don't get off our ass and do something now? Both sides are guilty of this. Both sides are so fearful of each other, that they'll only support somebody who the other side absolutely despises. When we vote based on memories and not on thinking, we end up with an election where nobody cares, and each side is a super villain of the other. To change our focus, we must change our thoughts. We must never rely on somebody else to make the change we want, we must get off our asses and make that change ourselves. Critical thought might be uncomfortable, but it is absolutely imperative." ☺

FROM THE MIND OF CRITIC
NOVEMBER 3rd 2016

From the mind of critic: "If we use it's raining like cats and dogs, bringing home the bacon, rule of thumb or getting gyped as part of our regular communication, but don't know where they came from, have we ever asked why? Do we just follow along with what we've always heard, because it has always been done so it must be the right thing? Or do we use these phrases, because we feel they best describe our emotions or actions? Many times when we're journeying into the unknown, we see examples of what people did before us. Sometimes we use them, because we don't know any better. These phrases might be completely innocent, or they might be completely vial. Of course we'd never know if we didn't think to ask, or simply didn't care to. Maybe if we thought about what our words mean, we'd think about what our actions mean. If we thought about our actions and who they affected and why, maybe the worst parts of our racist, sexist, homophobic, nationalistic, genocidal and murderous history wouldn't be repeated. Maybe we'd critically think about what we're saying and doing. Maybe we'd just plain think. Old sayings could describe the weather, wealth, demean a whole race, or what we could use to legally beat our wife. If we ask questions instead of blindly following, we'll find our positive and collective evolution will happen much easier." ☺

FROM THE MIND OF CRITIC
NOVEMBER 4th 2016

From the mind of critic: "If we read the directions when all attempts fail, do we feel like less of a person because we didn't figure it out ourselves? Do we believe that we must be strong, smart and courageous to succeed, and asking for help is admitting failure because we're weak, dumb and timid? Or do we think success doesn't mean we're the strongest, smartest or most-noble, but that we put ourselves in the right place at the right time without knowing it? Do we think asking for help when we don't know something, furthers our goals along? Many of us want to feel like we can do things all by ourselves. We've been trying to prove it since we were little kids. There comes a time when we grow out of this stage, and begin to realize that we don't know everything about everything. Maybe some of us never grew out of this teenage mindset. Maybe we know that we don't know something, but won't admit it. Maybe we don't want to be seen as less than. Maybe, just maybe we'll wake up one day and realize that we're imperfect human beings, who learn as we go. Maybe the sooner we realize that, the further along in our journey we'll be. If the true sign of knowledge is admitting there are many things we don't know, aren't we simply progressing forward when we ask for directions? While the word success is subjective, knowledge is not. Sometimes when we admit we don't have it, it actually proves that we do." ☺

FROM THE MIND OF CRITIC
NOVEMBER 8th 2016

From the mind of critic: "If we honestly believe that if we want something done right, we have to do it ourselves, do we honestly believe somebody else will do that same thing worse? Have we been let down by so many other people, that we've lost faith in humanity, causing us to float around trying to do as much as we can for ourselves before our time is up? Have we not allowed ourselves to fully open up to the world's possibilities, because we don't see the people that can help us, which causes us to spin out of control because we see all the millions of things we should be doing? Many times we're not used to doing things for our own betterment. We think others should do them, then get let down when they don't. Maybe we need to do some things for ourselves, and ask for help on others. Maybe being all one way or the other, is what got us in this mess in the first place. Maybe finding what we can do for ourselves, and finding out what others can do for us, is how we find out what we can do for others. Maybe this is how we discover the balance that will keep us motivated. Maybe through that balance is how we find out, that we do for ourselves, specifically so we can do for others. We all want to succeed, love and be loved. We all want to feel like we count and that we matter. Do we have to do for ourselves, yes. Do we have to let others do for us, yes. Do we have to prove to others that they can have faith in humanity, because we do?

There is no better feeling than overcoming adversity, or achieving a long term goal. We simply must remember that if we shun help from the world, success will never come. We allow success, by allowing the world to help." ☺

FROM THE MIND OF CRITIC
NOVEMBER 9th 2016

From the mind of critic: "What can we possibly say that would make election night make any sense? Is there a black and white explanation for electing such a despicable human being who lies so much, so often and so freely, he gives lying politicians a bad name? Or have we finally devolved to the point that we can't escape the complete destruction of the American system, before it's rebuilt and made better? I, like many us are a little numb. We could go on and on about how Bernie would have won, because he encompassed the same anger at the system that Trump did. We go on about how Bernie would have won simply because his name isn't Hillary Clinton, and people really hate her that much, and have for decades. We could even go on and on about how the misogynist and racist pig we now have as our president, is going to drive the great American experiment into the ground, losing all the gains we've made in the last 40 years, abortion will be made illegal, and the mass deportation force will round everybody up it thinks doesn't belong. We could do all that, throw up our hands while saying screw it, and completely give up. That's what they want us to do. They want us to have no hope for change, until we get slapped in the head with change that affects us. Not realizing that if we would've paid attention to the mountains of evidence, we wouldn't have had to get slapped, because we noticed what the problem was, and what built up to it.

Now is the time to prove our humanity. We can give up and say there's nothing we can do, or we can stand up, and never, ever sit down ever again. We choose our destiny, always. It can be built better, but only if we put in the effort." ☺

FROM THE MIND OF CRITIC
NOVEMBER 10th 2016

From the mind of critic: "Have the election results caused us to enter a brave new world, where everything we thought we knew about ourselves, our community, our country and our system is up in the air? Are all the freedoms, rights and opportunities we've come to expect living in the greatest country on the planet, going to disappear on the whim of a tyrant? Or are we simply in a transitional period in our collective evolution, where we're given a stark contrast of the paths in front of us, and we're given the choice of which one we want to travel? The entire world is taking a few deep breaths, wondering what the next six months will bring. We've always flirted with giving somebody power that has never had it before, just not somebody who so blatantly advocates blowing up the system. Many of us are angry with the way things are, and want to see major change. When this change involves blowing up the system however, are we ready to rebuild it? Were we even thinking about the rebuilding process when we talked about destruction? Clean slate thinking is dangerous. It's self-centered to want the world recreated in our image, making any detractors our enemies. There was talk before the new president-elect got his job, that when he took office, the revolution would start immediately. Well, where is it? Were we joking? Maybe we're trying to think up a way where our revolution won't bring on the same destruction that the other side wants.

Can we change things for the better, without completely tearing them down first? We can if we look forward, and only look backward for advice and strategy. Only thinking about memories is what got us into this mess, and wanting the past to come back. We must look forward and create the new future that will work for the best of us, not the worst of us." ☺

FROM THE MIND OF CRITIC
NOVEMBER 11th 2016

From the mind of critic: "If we're feeling depressed about electing the jokiest joke president of all time, is there any good that can be gleaned, the silver lining our grandma always told us about? Are there positive aspects of having all the racism, hate, xenophobia, homophobia and ignorance come to the surface after being suppressed for decades? Has all the emotion lingering since laws were passed in the 60s, and handed down from generation to generation, going to cause otherwise rational and critically thinking people to stick their heads in the sand and hide? It can be hard to find any positives, when we feel like we've been let down. It can also be an opportunity to get involved when we otherwise might not have. We could use this time to unleash positivity and love into the ether. If we're pragmatists, we'll see that whatever positivity we've felt in the past, we're now free to unleash it, because we finally realize it's our most powerful weapon. I went from numb, to feeling good because I realized what's actually important and what actually matters; which is being a good person and loving my neighbors. This is sorely lacking in our personal lives, which is why it reared its ugly head in our political lives. We can defeat anything if we stand up and love each other. We can squash all the hate and ignorance that rose in this election, until it cowers in the corner where it belongs. We have the power, will we finally use it?" ☺

FROM THE MIND OF CRITIC
NOVEMBER 13th 2016

From the mind of critic: "If we're the answer to all our prayers, but also our nightmares, how do we distinguish one from the other? Is there a definitive way to translate a good experience that might actually be a bad experience, or a bad experience that might actually be a good experience? Or since life is basically chaos, we're left to fend for ourselves, awash in a sea of who the hell am I, and what am I supposed to do? As we wake up and begin our daily routine, we might want to crawl back in bed because the thought of deciphering each and every event throughout the day, is such an insurmountable task that why should we even try. Every task seems insurmountable before we see what it entails. If we've never looked inside ourselves and seen what we really think, it can be scary. Thinking about our actions, and whether they are for our highest good or our lowest bad, gets easier with practice. Analyzation is how we find the right path. There might be black and white answers, but we still have to choose, by thinking about how we feel, and how it affects us and those around us. Once we realize there are no guarantees, black and white, one size fits all answers, we'll see what's good might be bad and vice versa. How do we figure out this predicament? We stay open and honest to what the universe has to offer, and let our light shine as brightly as we can. As long as we're consciously looking for answers, we're halfway to finding them." ☺

FROM THE MIND OF CRITIC
NOVEMBER 15th 2016

From the mind of critic: "If we can agree major change is underway, as well as collective evolution whether we want it to be or not, do we also agree everything has to be destroyed before it gets rebuilt? Do all the institutions we've grown up with, such as principles of justice, fairness and peace have to be reengineered, reorganized and utterly decimated before they can be re-constructed in such a way that hypocrisy becomes so obvious, that all of us will see it for what it really is, and stand up to stop it? Or can we keep tinkering, fiddling and hoping that ego and narcissism don't overshadow all the gains we've made over the last 150 years? Insider trading has always existed, as have laws against it. With all the deregulation in the last 20 years, officials started doing things out in the open, just to see if they could get away with them. Now, that experimental stage is over, and openly flaunting the rules has become the norm. Those of us who question these obvious deviations from a free society and free market, are seen as the trouble makers. When officials openly talk about how much they'll gain when they enter office, and then threaten to jail dissidents in for profit prisons that perpetuate the problem, we'll know we still have a lot of work to do. We all agree we need change, but if we clean our slate we will also clean out our soul. We might destroy the very goodness that made us human in the first place. Hypocrisy is our biggest enemy, not each other." ☺

FROM THE MIND OF CRITIC
NOVEMBER 16th 2016

From the mind of critic: "As more and more people keep asking how we could have elected the man we did, are those same people saying Hillary Clinton lost because she didn't appeal to white working class voters? Did she not appeal to all working class voters, or just white ones? If it is just the white ones, are they upset because the system has ignored the needs and wants of white America for too long? Are they upset America is getting too dark and too gay too quickly, and feel they're losing the supremacy they've held for years? Or is race and class so intertwined that you can't separate them, without ignoring what introduced each one? There are many reasons Hillary lost, she isn't likable, she isn't trustworthy, she isn't authentic, and she isn't one of us. The rage is much whiter on the right than the left, but the anger is the same. The downtrodden have been stepped on and lied to for so long, they'll support the first person that stands up for them. The danger comes when we're in this vulnerable state, and feel like we can't stand up ourselves. So we go toward that person who appeals to our emotions. Once we realize it's not so much white people needing more support, but all of us needing more support because we've been divided so long, we'll see that until we see each other as members of the same human family, race and class problems will persist.

Some people see dark days ahead, but never, ever forget that it's the darkest right before the dawn. Whatever our color or creed, the working people will have a say. Once we treat each other like humans and see each other in ourselves, most of our race and class problems will disappear. What do we have to lose?" ☺

FROM THE MIND OF CRITIC

NOVEMBER 17th 2016

From the mind of critic: "If we all want to love and be loved, do we all find it the same way? Do we have to completely give up, and think it's never going to happen before we're open enough? Must we reach a point where even thinking about love we don't have, causes so much pain we cry, until we say screw it, which also opens us up to let it in? Or is it all just chaos like life itself, and we have no control over any of it, except how kind we are to ourselves? As we get older, many of us will have kids and families of our own, carrying on the lineage that our parents may or may not have handed down to us. For those of us who are single, we can see all of these relationships going on around us, and wonder when it's going to be our time. It's hard to see people that seem to have found that person, when we haven't. Once we realize that it's better to be in no relationship than a bad one, we'll see that maybe we haven't found that relationship yet, because we aren't willing to settle. Maybe we're looking for something real, because we know the soul, spirit and heart connection involved, and we aren't willing to waste our time on anything less. Loneliness is hard, especially when we let it get the best of us. We might have a heart connection with somebody, but for some reason it wasn't the right time. What we must never do is lose sight of this connection, and give it the full benefit of the doubt. If it doesn't work out, at least we know we tried.

Some of us haven't found love yet, and some of us have but haven't been allowed to let it fully blossom. Love will happen, and chances are it will be greater than anything we ever imagined." ☺

FROM THE MIND OF CRITIC
NOVEMBER 18th 2016

From the mind of critic: "If there really aren't stupid questions, how come some inquiries clog up the system, and completely halt forward progress? Are these questions asked by people who actually want to know the answer, because they don't know something? Is the judgement of the question itself being stupid, all in the mind of the judger who thinks somebody should know something, that they might not? Or are these progress cloggers meant to do a specific thing, with their askers 100% fully aware of what they're doing? Many concepts in life are definable, with easily comprehendible meanings. Other concepts are completely subjective, with definitions that can and often do utterly change depending on our beliefs and life experiences. Similar to love, hate, anger and misery, stupidity is something that means one thing to one person, and something else to another. Questions aren't stupid if somebody wants to gain information they don't have. If somebody asks questions to clog up progress in their personal lives or in politics it isn't stupid either, it's simply strategy. If there's something we don't like or don't agree with, it doesn't mean it's stupid, it's simply something that we don't like or don't agree with. Asking questions and not blindly following, is imperative for our positive and collective evolution. Pre-judging is detrimental to the whole process of evolving past the bullshit, that has kept us down for generations.

To solve problems, we need to fully describe how and why they're happening. Questions and thoughts are never stupid, they're just different. To succeed we simply need to get over ourselves." ☺

FROM THE MIND OF CRITIC
NOVEMBER 21st 2016

From the mind of critic: "If faces come out of the rain when we're strange, are we strange to ourselves, or others? Do the faces that appear judge something they don't understand, somebody who appears strange to them? Or are these faces ignorant of what they don't know about, and feel generalizations make the best descriptions? Sometimes as we journey through our day, we aren't quite sure who we are. Sometimes we come into contact with many wolves in sheep's clothing, who appear extremely sure of who we are. We take advice as the gospel, because we haven't given much thought to who we are. Maybe we believe this person, because they sound like they know what they're talking about. Maybe we 've given so much thought to who we are, that most advice comes off as the ravings as of an ignorant, uneducated lunatic, who is so confident about their knowledge, they don't realize that a four year old could poke holes through their bullshit. Once we realize that there will always be people out there who are overly confident about their knowledge, we'll see that the only judgement that matters is ours of ourselves. As long as we aren't strange to ourselves, most people won't see us as strange. Once we have that confidence in ourselves, the fiercest of ignorance will never break through.

Faces will always come out of the rain whether we feel strange or not, how we react to them depends on how much we love ourselves." ☺

FROM THE MIND OF CRITIC
NOVEMBER 22nd 2016

From the mind of critic: "If comedians, comedic TV shows, skit comedy shows, late night shows and satirists are overflowing with a tsunami of material that keeps getting taller, stronger and deeper as the people in power get more ridiculous, is it a good thing? Is it a good thing that it's so easy to make fun of people at the top? Is it easier to act against day to day hypocrisy, when we laugh at it first? Or is our society, humanity and decency on the decline because making fun is easy? Does it prove that the easier it is to lob insults and tell jokes, the worse we're collectively devolving? Laughter is the best medicine is an old cliché for a reason. If we can't laugh at ourselves and where we have to improve, serious doubt creeps in as to whether our humanity really is on the decline. Sometimes we're so messed up that we have to laugh, or we'd cry. Once we realize that laughter is a coping skill and an educational skill, and often simultaneously, we'll see comedy is made for all sorts of reasons, that serve all sorts of agendas. When we do learn to laugh including but not exclusively about ourselves, we'll see that once we're in a positive mood, we're way more likely to not only take positive action, but ascertain the facts that would spur action. Laughter is as much medicine as it is motivation. May we always applaud those who make that concept easier to understand." ☺

FROM THE MIND OF CRITIC
NOVEMBER 23rd 2016

From the mind of critic: "If rules are meant to be broken, what's the point of having them in the first place? Are they simply guidelines that attempt to reign in bad behavior? Do they allow people to go right to the line of illegal acts, and even a little past, because people always break the law, but are stopped from going too far? Are rules meant to stop bad behavior, but because rule makers are human, those with vast financial capabilities can break all the rules and never go to jail? Does this cause those of us with no financial capabilities to languish in jail, because we have no way to pay off rule makers? Is this what allows financially able individuals to buy off lawmakers in the first place? Without rules, chaos becomes a much bigger possibility. Fairness must bleed through the whole system, or we can make all the laws and rules we want, but they won't mean a damn thing if they only apply to some of us. Politicians play fast and loose with the truth, before and after they get their "paid for" desired position. It's no wonder they so openly flout the rules meant to stop them from accepting payoffs from others to gain influence, because it's how they got their position in the first place. Let's get one thing straight, when the president does something illegal, it's still illegal. When the president has a conflict of interest, it's still a conflict of interest. Are we going to allow a fascist to tear up everything good about America? Are we going to stand up and do something?" ☺

FROM THE MIND OF CRITIC
NOVEMBER 24th 2016

From the mind of critic: "If kindness, gratitude, love and presence in the moment are the only authentic methods to move us forward, how come so many of us shy away from them? Are we afraid that if we show any vulnerability we'll be viewed as week, and people will walk all over us, making their way forward much easier? Or have we never known the power of gratitude and kindness and the motivational power it contains? Do we believe the only way to get ahead, is to be the biggest jerk we can to as many people as we can? Doing something we've never done before or don't have much experience at is hard. It can cause us to second guess every action and thought we have. If our first reaction is to be a jerk because we've seen other people succeed that way, we're moving forward with what examples we've seen. We can fake it till we make it, but it's more than that. Maybe we're afraid to show gratitude and kindness too early, for fear we won't be defensive enough when our detractors come knocking. Do we only deserve kindness if we're successful? How can we be thankful for anything unless it's the 100% completion of our dreams? Once we realize that our failure is guaranteed if we wait until we have everything we want to be grateful and kind, we'll see that gratitude for all we have, and kindness to ourselves and others, is how we stay present in the moment, making it possible to move forward.

It's not so much about others pushing us forward so we push ourselves, it's about loving ourselves and others, which is the only thing that continuously and infinitely pushes us forward." ☺

FROM THE MIND OF CRITIC
NOVEMBER 25th 2016

From the mind of critic: "If the best things in life are free, does it mean all good things in life are also free? Does the mere fact that money is exchanged for goods and services automatically make it bad, because monetary gain is the main motivation, and not an actual want to do something positive? Or does it come down to a persons' intent, and if somebody wants to tear down or build up they will, whether money is involved or not? Is love, happiness, fulfillment, usefulness and gratitude free, because we can't fully define something that's subjective, just like hate, darkness, persecution, denigration and weakness of will? Maybe we strive throughout our day to define and appraise what we see, simply to make sense of the chaos. The line between what we know is good for our soul, and what we know will continuously drag us down will be blurred. Maybe the determining factor between what's good, and great, has nothing to do with money. Maybe it has everything to do with our physical, emotional and spiritual survival. Until we reach a point in our personal evolution where we see each other as human beings that have the same needs, and can barter with each other once again, money will always be a factor. Until that time, we must see how we can help people for the sake of helping them. Good and great things will be drawn to us when we're kind to others, which starts with us being kind to ourselves." ☺

FROM THE MIND OF CRITIC
NOVEMBER 26th 2016

From the mind of critic: "If we want to escape what's in front of us because we don't like what we see, is it the same as using our imagination to imagine something better? Do we escape into our imagination because what we see is so terrible, that we have to escape for our physical well-being? Do we escape because what we see isn't necessarily bad or good, but we want to keep positively evolving? Do we use our imaginations to usher in hope, caring, tolerance, acceptance, accountability, humanism and badly needed love into a community, a system, and a world that needs all it can get if it wants to survive long into the future? Ignorance is bred by ignoring what's right in front of our face for years, and feeling threatened because we don't know something. This happens specifically because we've ignored it for so long. This can cause us to escape, and picture a better world where we're infinitely happier. If our imagination is spurred by dark thoughts about what we don't like, our imagination will make us picture a world that only benefits us, our inner circle, and people that think, look and act like us. If our imagination is spurred by what we do like, we'll be driven to create a world that is loving, caring, satisfying and fulfilling for all of us. Specifically because this imaginative version of a new world came from a positive place, we'll feel so good we'll want to share it with others, so they can experience it as well.

Whether escaping our imagination or imagining our escape, or simply imagining a world where we no longer have to escape, if we come from collective uplift and not self-preservation, the outcome will be better than we ever imagined." ☺

FROM THE MIND OF CRITIC

NOVEMBER 29th 2016

From the mind of critic: "If we don't believe the Beatles when they said love is all we need, have we ever injected as much love into the system as would be needed to make an honest determination? Is it a matter of love having no monetary value, and we need money to pay our bills? Is it a failure to see that when we start from love and gratitude, success sprouts? Most true meanings get lost among cherry picking what sounds good, and repeating what we've heard, which is usually void of context. To get the real meaning, we must ask what the whole line or phrase is, and what real world applications it contains. Love is really all we need, it's all we need to begin our journey, because it's the place all smart, just and peaceful thoughts spring from. Once we create actions that bring us the joy and success we crave, we'll see we don't have to regret anything if we start with love. The whole concept of needing other things besides love, or that love is all we need misses the point. Love makes all things possible, it opens our heart and mind so we can move forward in a way that's for our highest good. Love is the only thing we need, because it's where most things come from. They can come from hate, which usually ends up with terribly tragic results. Love is not the end of the journey, or something only collected along the way; it's where the journey begins. If we don't start correctly, how can we expect to go in the right direction?" ☺

FROM THE MIND OF CRITIC
NOVEMBER 30th 2016

From the mind of critic: "If the answer to our prayers is praying for answers, are we admitting defeat before the game even starts? Are we letting go of any hope to get where we want to go? Do we think that to achieve our dreams, goals and aspirations, we have to let somebody do it for us? Have we let go of the notion that we can do everything ourselves, specifically so others can push us past where we'd get alone, and in ways we didn't expect? Admitting we need human contact to survive, is tough if we've always been told to pull ourselves up by our bootstraps. How are we supposed to ask for help, when we've been told that if we wanted something done right, we had to do it ourselves? If we still can't do it right, are we a failure? If we believe that asking for help opens us up to other possibilities and perspectives, are we simply too lazy to do the action ourselves, so we let others do the work? In life, being an honest person can be hard, trial and error is the only way to discover when we need help, and when we need to do things solo. Nothing is black and white, or one size fits all. We're unique, and have different definitions of what balance means in our lives. We simply need to remember, it's never all one way or the other. If we never do anything, we're assured defeat. Answers to prayers can come from anywhere, we stay open to their possibilities by critically thinking about what's in front of us, and its context." ☺

FROM THE MIND OF CRITIC
DECEMBER 1st 2016

From the mind of critic: "If we go in through the out-door or out through in-door, are we carving our own path many of us have dreamed of, but very few have carried out? Does fear hold us back from going our own way, an unseen force that will squash us the moment we step out of line? Or do we forget about clearing our own path because our critical thinking skills are working overtime, and organizing our thoughts is as far as we've ever gotten? When it actually comes time to design, chart and then walk our own path, do we have any energy left? Taking too much time to organize and plan can prevent us from taking action. We might feel planning is the action, whether we're choosing our own path or not. If we're delving into the unknown, we must remember that we have nothing to fear but fear itself. Fear comes from us, and whatever we perceive, which is the ultimate self-roadblock. We can paralyze ourselves with a zillion variables, or zero variables depending on how we see the unknown. If people have ever told us to get over ourselves, it's simply an inarticulate way of saying we should get out of our own way. Whatever door, window or path we choose, success will find us if we're open and honest about what's in front of us, and about our self-sabotage. Doors will always open for us, when we pull the keys out of our pocket." ☺

FROM THE MIND OF CRITIC

DECEMBER 2nd 2016

From the mind of critic: "If we demand respect, humanism, accountability and transparency of our elected officials, but then fail to live up to those ideals ourselves, how can we expect things to get any better? If we expect all the change to come from the outside instead of the inside, are we like a dog chasing its tail? Do we think that if change is made by someone else, then we don't have to? Or are we simply looking for the right example to drive us down the correct path, and just need a jump start? We've all heard the Gandhi quote we have to be the change we want to see. If the world seems dark, where something terrible and despicable pops out around every corner, it may seem like there's no positivity or humanity left, and ego and narcissism have taken over. This is when it's most important to be a good person, filling ourselves with love, beauty and kindness, and spreading it to everybody. This can be difficult if we've never done it before. The more we do it though, it turns from something abnormal, into just something we do. At any time during this trial and error period we see some people who guide us, and some who try to steer us off track. We must surround ourselves with people who build us up. When we do, we see all the outcroppings of what it can create. As long as we demand respect, humanism, accountability and transparency of ourselves, the people we elect will reflect who we actually are, instead of a false picture we've constructed." ☺

FROM THE MIND OF CRITIC
DECEMBER 4th 2016

From the mind of critic: "If the mind is a terrible thing to waste, how come we waste it on trivial matters more often than not? Do we even know the meaning of the things we say? Do we simply repeat what we've always heard, without giving a second thought to its context? Or do we know the meanings of our most used phrases, and see how they could apply to our lives and others, but don't take action because that's below us, and only meant for the little people who run like little ants from job to job as we laugh, because they think phrases alone give them a chance? Language is one of those funny things that matter, and doesn't matter at the same time. The way we express thoughts and ideas isn't as important as the fact that we express them in the first place. Whether or not we know the meaning of what we say, it always has a meaning, context and after-effect. None of us are above words, phrases or context we or may not be trying to portray. Which is one of the exact reasons we must build others up, not tear them down to persecute and control them; which is the ultimate waste because the gains are temporary, no matter how permanent they seem. Critical thought is vital to our existence and continued survival. If this critical thought is spent tearing others down and taking advantage of them, we're not only wasting our mind, but wasting yet one more opportunity to make the world better than we found it.

Critical thought will lead us to what's important. It must be our choice to use that knowledge for the positive and collective good. That's how we don't waste our mind, but preserve it." ☺

FROM THE MIND OF CRITIC
DECEMBER 6th 2016

From the mind of critic: "If one man shoots another man and gets arrested, charged and tried, not to mention held without bail till that trial starts to ensure attendance, while another man shoots a different man during extremely similar circumstances, but gets released soon after being arrested with no charges, do we still believe the justice system is fair? Do we believe a road rage incident involving one black man shooting another black man needs to be tried, investigated and stopped, because it's the exact problem that's causing the downfall of society? Do we believe a road rage incident involving a white man shooting a black man needs to be tried, investigated and stopped because it's the exact problem causing the downfall of society? Or do we find ourselves in the middle, believing everything should be investigated, but realize that fear of the other however unjustified, has been learned, inherited and imbedded for generations, and causes some of us to shoot people who may not necessarily look like us? No matter what side of the political spectrum we find ourselves on, we could all agree we have many issues that have been kicked down the road for others to deal with. Maybe we do this because it's hard to look at ourselves, and ask what we as a society have done to prevent and/or cause this. Maybe we don't do anything about racial issues, because then we'd have to admit there's a problem.

Maybe we shouldn't believe everything that anybody says, and take everything from everybody with a grain of salt. Maybe we'll realize that letting go of issues and attitudes that don't serve us, entails recognizing the problem so we know we're letting go of the right thing. We'll see that recognition is done when bad events happen, not after the fact. Once we see that shooting people is bad, we'll see that putting ourselves in the shoes of the victim, might make us less lenient on the shooters. Peace on earth involves peace for all of us, and listening when people say they don't have peace, even if we think they do." ☺

FROM THE MIND OF CRITIC
DECEMBER 7th 2016

From the mind of critic: "If we can't do what ten people tell us to do, do we end up remaining the same? Do we try to make a list of all that advice that comes in, delete the bad, keep the good, and move down the list, checking issues off as we go along? Or do we hear it all, try to take it all in, and instead of moving down the list doing things one at a time, we think of everything at once which causes our mind to spin out of control to the point where the only way to stop it, is to do nothing? Many of the people we interact with on a daily basis mean well, some don't, but most do. When they see our lives, thoughts, actions and plans they might have an idea of how to do it more efficiently, clearly and with less stress. Sometimes those methods are good, sometimes the people just think they're good, or that they're good for them. Sometimes the same methods are repeated by many people, which might make us take a closer look. We must always stay vigilant as to what we want, what we feel and what we would like to see. So when somebody gives us vague advice that really doesn't help at all, we won't lose ourselves amongst the fog of self-doubt and sabotage. Once we realize that it's not so much about doing everything people say, but critically thinking about what they say, we'll see that being honest with ourselves about who we are and what we want, allows us to keep what works for us, and stops us from spinning out of control.

We can't do what everybody says, and everybody can't do everything we say, but if we listen, we'll see where we hurt each other, and where we help. If we're not here to help, what are we here for really?" ☺

FROM THE MIND OF CRITIC
DECEMBER 8th 2016

From the mind of critic: "If racism, sexism, homophobia and other ignorant and unconscious beliefs are learned not born, why do some of us learn them and immediately disassociate, disavow, and extricate this darkness because we recognize them for the destructive force they are? Do some of us never think to question these lessons because it's the way things have always been, and there's a certain comfort in that? Do some of us pick up critical thinking skills sooner than others, so we're able to utilize them sooner? Or do some of us never pick up critical thinking skills because nobody around us has them, and so not only have we never learned them, we've never even seen how they can be applied to better our lives? Media, social networking and all forms of communication are great opportunities to test our critical thinking. Which can also further imbed our opinions, because they come across as all knowing; especially if we don't pay attention to what's going on, which makes the media sound like they know what they're talking about, whether they actually do or not. There are a lot of messages which bombard us all the time. Some we've heard for a long time about how a certain person or group thinks, acts, or looks different than us. We become scared because they must be scheming against us, and screw them for doing that, which is where hate introduces itself.

Once we realize that by simply asking why we feel a certain way, or why somebody else feels the way they do that it upends the oldest paradigm, we'll see that 99% of ignorant and hateful beliefs, statements and thoughts are based on blindly following. Hate is based on being blind to what's real, and love is based on being open to what's real. And isn't real and make believe a concept we should have learned watching cartoons as a kid?" ☺

FROM THE MIND OF CRITIC
DECEMBER 9th 2016

From the mind of critic: "If politicians continually look to enrich themselves as they gain experience, is it because the rest of us also look to enrich ourselves as we gain experience? Does all the game playing, lying and scheming that politicians do affect how we go about our daily lives? Or does all our game playing, lying and scheming affect how politicians go about their daily lives? Whether we affect politics more than politics affects us, is hard to determine given our current climate. More people are paying attention to what's going on, have thoughts and questions about our political system, and about the leaders we've elected. If all the questions aren't followed up by actions however, because the questions are thought to be actions, then nothing is going to change because questions can be deferred, and actions can't. When action is taken, it can be ignored but only for so long, until reaction is a guarantee. When questions are asked but not followed up on, they can be ignored until people forget about their importance. Once we realize that the games we play and the games politicians play are the same games, we'll see that politicians might have much more money, power and influence than us, but if we had the same money, power and influence, we'd do the same thing. Politicians are human, just like the population. If we want them to be less evil and corrupt, we must be less evil and corrupt.

Politicians aren't different from us, they are us. Being the change we want to see will not only change our lives, but will filter throughout the entire planet. It all starts with us being kind." ☺

FROM THE MIND OF CRITIC
DECEMBER 10th 2016

From the mind of critic: "If bringing people together is so difficult, so above and beyond anything we believe is possible, how come when real truth is spoken, people always gather round? Are we waiting for that one person, or that one thing that truly speaks to our soul to introduce itself? Or are we so worn out from the system being so phony for so long, we'll follow anything that sounds remotely positive? We're all random individual snowflakes, moving about in the fog trying to make sense of chaos, and finding and carving out our little corner so we can survive. We're also all human beings that want to leave a mark, to take care of ourselves and our family, to be good people, to count, to matter and to have purpose. We're all different, and we're all the same. When we journey forward whether consciously or unconsciously, we're looking for help, guides, signs and symbols that will help explain the world. Sometimes we get divided by a power structure that has been in power for thousands of years, and knows it's losing its grip. Sometimes we gather because we just can't take the bullshit anymore. Sometimes we band together because our previous conceptions about religion, race, gender and sexual orientation, pale in comparison to the importance of building the world we want to see, and not just endlessly talking about it.

Sometimes we let go of our ignorance long enough to see, that the only thing holding us back from rising up and throwing off our shackles, is us. We've all been lied to, but we've also been told a lot of truths. We simply have to open our eyes and ears, so our heart can take in all the love and beauty of the world; even if our mind has tricked us into thinking it isn't there. It is there, we just have to use it for collective uplift, because it's the only true motivation." ☺

FROM THE MIND OF CRITIC
DECEMBER 13th 2016

From the mind of critic: "If we walk by a disheveled, sunburnt, unshaven, dirty clothed, dirty faced and foul smelling person on a street corner begging for change and think there but for the grace of god, go I, is it because we think we have no control over our upward mobility? Do we believe God, spirit or some other outside force is the determining factor between us being devoid of the physical, mental and financial attributes it takes to be a contributing member of society? Or do we know all the hard work and struggle that we've put in just to get to place we're at, even if it is barely enough to get by; and know all our forward progress can be taken away on the whim of a power broker? Times are tough, hard work alone doesn't get us as far as it used to be, there aren't as many jobs. Companies love to move their operations overseas because they know American workers will never work for $100 a month. These are statements we all could agree with, no matter what side of the political spectrum we find ourselves on. Some of us still believe that it's all out of our hands, that no matter what we do, how hard we work or push for progress, an all knowing force is the only one that says who is homeless and who isn't, and who is successful and who isn't. Maybe we believe it can all be taken away either by captains of religion, or captains of industry.

Maybe some of us work hard knowing success can be taken away but do it anyway, because we know sometimes it isn't taken. Sometimes we discover we still have the ability to surprise ourselves. Whether it is the grace of God or the grace of fascists, life is short and temporary. As long as we put our full effort forward, we should never, ever feel ashamed. None of us are ever above anybody else." ☺

FROM THE MIND OF CRITIC
DECEMBER 14th 2016

From the mind of critic: "If there is always light at the end of the tunnel, if it's always coldest and darkest before the dawn, is it mandatory that it be cold, dark and strenuous before the light? Are we required by the unwritten rules of the universe to endure hardships, adversity, persecution, extreme odds and danger before we're even considered worthy of the light? Or do all of us deserve light, but some of us just have harder and more extreme paths to get there? Gaining motivation to push us forward on our journey can be quite an accomplishment, until we figure out sustaining that motivation is more challenging, because it's how we enact many of the goals we attempt to describe. Sometimes we hit roadblocks that are placed from the outside and some from the inside, but this is when picturing the light overpowering the darkness is most useful. If we don't picture the good times and how they have been, and most importantly how they will be implemented, how do we ever expect to make it through the bad times? All of us have the blues from time to time, that's normal. We all have our crosses to bare and our battles to fight, it's how we react to them that matters. We could get lost in the darkness and be swallowed up. We could push through because the slivers of light we see when we're paying attention, are examples of what's to come.

We might believe that light only exists amongst the darkness, and if we feel light during times that aren't completely terrible, it must be fake. Many of us have lessons to learn so we can be open, honest and conscious people. We simply have varying degrees of darkness we must overcome, which appear in infinite ways. We must never put somebody down if they're further behind in the process than us. To create light, we have to be light. It will attract others, and prove we don't need the end of a tunnel. We could be living in light right now. It is our choice, we just have to figure out if light or dark will fulfill our dreams." ☺

FROM THE MIND OF CRITIC
DECEMBER 15th 2016

From the mind of critic: "If the world doesn't revolve around us, who does it revolve around? Is the fact that we create our own reality, mean we create our own world, which in turn means our world revolves around us, just like everybody else's world revolves around them? Or does the world simply revolve around the sun, and any attempt to correlate it to our emotional and mental maturity, is like putting human names, faces, characteristics, personalities and aspirations on animal cartoon characters; basically a way to make them more easily relatable to our daily lives? We've all heard from family, friends, coworkers or romantic partners that we aren't the center of the universe, and the world doesn't revolve around us. While this might be done to tap down our ego, it can also have an extremely negative effect if we don't take it the next step. Once we realize that creating our own reality means creating our own destiny, we'll see that the next step is unique for all of us. It involves finding our place, purpose and passion, which can only happen when we see that we're the center of our universe. Being centered and grounded is how we find our place in the microcosm. The universe doesn't revolve around us, specifically because it's made up of our individual universes'. If we fail to see this collective struggle as what unites us in the idea that we're all the same, we won't see how we're interconnected.

We won't see how our success is tied to everybody else's financial, mental, and moral success. The world might not revolve around us, but the world does revolve around ALL of us." ☺

FROM THE MIND OF CRITIC
DECEMBER 16th 2016

From the mind of critic: "If Jews and Muslims are so different, how come their countless commonalities are pushed aside in favor of their few differences? If Blacks and Whites, Mexicans and Whites, Asians and Whites, Arabs and Whites, Muslims and Hindus, Muslims and Christians, Jews and Christians, Muslims and Buddhists, Hindus and Buddhists, Americans and Europeans, Americans and Africans, Africans and Europeans, Middle Easterners and Africans, Gays and Straights, Young and Old, if we're all so different, how come we focus on the 10% of things we don't agree on, instead of the 90% of things we do? Is it because it's what we've always done, and we've grown comfortable even though we know it's detrimental to our personal evolution? Do we stay with what we know, instead of what is unknown even if we know we'd benefit? Or do we keep using old stereotypes because we believe they're true? If we won't admit that we believe in stereotypes, are we blinding ourselves and holding up progress? There are a million different reasons which differ from person to person as to why we focus on our differences, instead of our sames. Maybe we're scared of what we don't know, which turns into hate because we think these people who don't look, act or believe like us are out to do us harm. Maybe we're not used to interacting, let alone conversing with people on the other side of the political and/or religious spectrum than us.

Maybe we know change is hard, and that it's so much easier to say something once in a while, before going back to the same old thing. Once we realize that our different ethnicities, looks, religions, sexual preferences and politics are what makes us unique, not different, we'll see that we might all have different paths to the light, but it's the same light. I could go down the list of all the similarities of supposed opposing groups, but it would take a book in and of itself. I'll just say that most generational and imbedded conflicts can be solved, by realizing we all want to be loved, respected and honored. Once we understand this, only then can we flip the conversation to start from where we agree, and work and evolve from there." ☺

FROM THE MIND OF CRITIC
DECEMBER 20th 2016

From The Mind Of Critic: "If we believe the world would be a lot better off if everybody spoke their mind, and were truthful about their emotions, are we prepared for the outcome? Will we battle with others who we don't agree with until one of us falls, making our issues 10 times worse because we hid them for so long? Or just as in the five stages of grief, will we eventually come to acceptance because we were able to honestly express ourselves to each other, not how we think would cause less conflict? Honesty and trust are the biggest things in any relationship whether between lovers, friends, families, communities or governments. Maybe we don't trust the government because we don't trust each other. We could be completely honest when expressing ourselves, but if we're not listening to the other side we'll simply be waiting for our turn to talk, which won't solve anything. Letting go of what doesn't serve us is only possible when we're honest with ourselves, and to collectively let go of things that have been plaguing us for generations, we must recognize them first. Talking and listening only work in tandem." ☺

FROM THE MIND OF CRITIC
DECEMBER 21st 2016

From the mind of critic: If uttering Happy Holidays during the month of December is how we recognize all cultures, how come the imagery behind the words tell a different story? If Christmas trees, songs, outfits, music, cookies, wreaths, holly and Santa are the background, are we trying to obscure what we really want to say? Are we giving the ultimate in token responses by making it sound like we're supportive, while also making it abundantly obvious what religion we are? Being proud of our culture and where we came from, is never a bad thing. We can run into trouble however, when we think our culture is better than all other cultures. We may think any representation of another culture is an attack on our own, even if it is no more than two simple words. This may cause us to insert as much of our culture in, just shy of saying the actual words. There is no more a war on Christmas, then a war on Hanukah or Kwanzaa. People want to be heard and feel like they matter, just like we do. To throw off the shackles of being fake because we think it's the only way to succeed, we must be honest in our speech. Meaning, the words Merry Christmas should be the only ones with Christmas imagery behind it; while the words Happy Holidays should only include images of all holidays. We are either inclusive people, or we're not. Infinite conflict is assured with half-truths and miniscule efforts. Infinite peace is assured if we bare the authenticity of our soul.

Say Merry Christmas if you really mean Merry Christmas, and say Happy Holidays if you really mean Happy Holidays. Just don't say bullshit and dress it up as roses, it will devolve us all." ☺

FROM THE MIND OF CRITIC
DECEMBER 22nd 2016

From the mind of critic: "If we finally have a chance to let go of what doesn't serve us, and hasn't for eons, will we take it? Will the letting go process get stifled, because it involves recognizing each and every thing we want to let go of? Is it too much for us to take, because it slaps us in the face with every problem we've ever kicked down the road? Will we roll with the punches because we have to deal with uncomfortable things? Donald Trump becoming our 45th president was a surprise to some, and not to others. The division in this country doesn't fall along party lines. It falls on realists, and fakeists. Those of us who see what's going on in front of our face without partisan lenses, and those of us who view life through rose colored glasses. I'm not going to argue with people who think the world is 6000 years old, and that the 50s were great for everybody. We've made it this far in our evolution of race and class, but we're only halfway. Just because we have a black president, gay marriage and medical pot in 25 states, doesn't mean problems have disappeared. It means problems have evolved into a racist, bigoted and religious force putting Trump into office, because they fight tooth and nail against any positive change. I realize not everyone who voted for him is a racist and bigot, but you can't tell me they didn't believe most of what he said. If they did, they're being disproven tenfold before he even takes office, filling the swamp to capacity rather than draining it.

The unconstitutional corruption that is about to permeate every nook and cranny of government, is a turning point for all of us. Will we actually see what's going on in front of our face and act on that, or some blind and dark partisan fantasy we've built up in our heads? Our bright or bleak future depends on it." ☺

FROM THE MIND OF CRITIC

DECEMBER 23rd 2016

From the mind of critic: "If we're more loving, tolerant, caring, peaceful and giving this time of year, why is that? Do we feel some kind of warmth that smothers us in so many cookies, decorations and eggnog that we have to share it with others, so they can feel it too? Or do we spread more joy this time of year, because we see how much we've neglected it during our entire year's interactions, and we have to play catch up? There's so much to be thankful for, so much beauty and so many good people, it's easy to find the light if we try. At the same time, there is so much darkness, that it will bleed into everything we see, hear, touch, smell and sense if we let it. Maybe certain things are hard if we've never done them before, or haven't had much practice. The more we do things, the better we get. The more we treat others like we'd like to be treated, and remind ourselves that we're all in this together, the less abnormal and weird it will feel around the holidays. This time of year is filled with much joy, wonder and love. There is no better feeling in the world, except feeling that way all year long. Think of how many problems we could solve, we literally have nothing to lose. Except negativity and hate, and who wouldn't want to lose that?" ☺

FROM THE MIND OF CRITIC
DECEMBER 24th 2016

From the mind of critic: "If this is the season of our discontent, couldn't it also be the season of our contentment? Do signs point to the destruction of how we think, feel and act, completely changing the fabric of who we are and the trajectory of our evolution? Or have signs and symbols always pointed in different directions, and we can choose to see them as driving us downhill, or as simply driving us in an unexpected direction, where we see the opportunity to make the positive changes we've always dreamed of? The overt changes we face haven't been this blatant since the 60s. The possibilities for wholesale change within our system of government and how we conduct ourselves as a country, are extremely high. Presidential rules are being thrown out the window on a whim and a tweet. Conflicts of interest are disappearing as a concept. Multiple departments of government could be eliminated, causing vast swaths of basic life functions to be privatized. Press freedoms could be squashed, ushering in definitive fascism. The extreme far right's dreams coming true, gives us an opportunity to make the positive changes we've always imagined. The ugliness, hate and divisiveness that has always simmered under the surface, is now on the surface and can be finally smacked down. We must utilize this chance to stand up and fight for what we believe in, because the vault of power that has held sway for eons knows it's losing its grip.

Life is all about perception, how we view people and events. Do we picture ourselves living within a fascist state, or a truly democratic one? Our future is up to us, do we want to create or destroy, it's as simple as that." ☺

FROM THE MIND OF CRITIC
DECEMBER 27th 2016

From the mind of critic: "If we don't know what's truly possible until we try, why don't we try to convince ourselves we do before we try? Are we trying to get an idea of what's possible by getting words of wisdom from others, while also accounting for our strengths and weaknesses to make an educated guess? Do we hear advice but obsess over weaknesses, forgetting about our strengths and what we've accomplished, which makes us think we aren't good enough? We don't know what it means to surprise ourselves, until we realize we have the ability. We constantly analyze and reanalyze our thoughts and actions. Too much over thinking takes away positives, leaving bad to linger after all other possibilities are exhausted. Some analyzation is good however, because it reminds us of how good we have it, and what's possible when we get out of our own way. Finding balance between over analyzing and negativity, and under analyzing and negativity, is hard. Just like anything though, we get better with practice. Once we find the goldilocks zone of analyzing, we'll see that not only can we surprise ourselves, but we can also move the goalposts as to what's possible. Trying something new is hard because we're experiencing the unknown. It becomes much less scary when we see experimentation as the process of moving forward, which is always better than over analyzing and moving backward, right?" ☺

FROM THE MIND OF CRITIC

DECEMBER 28th 2016

From the mind of critic: "If money only exists as a concept because we put our faith in it, but it's also the root of all evil, does evil only exist because we put our faith in it? Does goodness only exist because we put our faith in it? Or do both goodness and evil exist only because we put our faith in them equally, and would both disappear if we favored one over the other? It's amazing the things we get so hung up on, because of the real world applications of them slapping us in the face. Paper and plastic money allow us to go, do and buy things that seem real, but lose their validity when we realize we could be using shells and rocks for currency. Evil exists because we feed it, ignore its buildup and then blame the other side when it explodes. Maybe we thought being too good made us weak, so to defeat the dark side we had to become part of the dark side. Maybe we thought being evil made us strong, so to hang on to this fleeting power, we became more evil until we mutated into the people we always fought against. Once we fully realize what "we create our own reality" really means, we'll see that if we believe something is real, it is; just like if we believe something isn't real. If there are positive changes we want to make, we must have faith and believe in that better world. The positive world we imagine becomes a reality through every thought and action we take, whether we're cognizant of it or not.

Being the change we want to see, starts with us believing and having faith in positive change. We just have to remember what's for our highest good, is also for everyone else's. We all succeed when we all picture that positive world existing." ☺

FROM THE MIND OF CRITIC

DECEMBER 29th 2016

From the mind of critic: "If we constantly and repeatedly ask why can't we all get along, and then don't follow it up with positive action, are we trying to have our cake and eat it too? Are we trying to take credit and praise for simply uttering words, hoping somebody else will take action, citing us as their primary motivation? Or do we realize it starts with ideas, which become words, which in turn spurn actions, and we're just trying to do our small part to get the ball rolling in the right direction? We all want to do something important and feel like we matter during our short time on this earth. Finding our voice can be hard, especially if we've never allowed our positive thoughts to surface before. The benefits of creating a positive reality are huge. Constantly articulating a problem can raise awareness, bringing people around to show them we can't be silenced. Although, if all we do is articulate the problem without actually doing the actions we speak of, then nothing will change. To crush negativity and usher in the collective and conscious evolution we all know is upon us, we must take bold, unapologetic and positive action. To take action we must have ideas, which are spawned by words. Once we realize our purpose starts but doesn't end with words, we'll see a whole world filled with possibilities. We just have to get out of our own way." ☺

FROM THE MIND OF CRITIC
DECEMBER 30th 2016

From the mind of critic: "If we feel great that we've found our passion, but are lonely, do we realize the alone time can give us the time we need to work our passion? Does the loneliness we feel overshadow all the joy we've gained from not only finding our passion, but working it as well, making us forget what's really important? Or even though we're well acquainted with these lonely feelings, we see how they can drag us down, so we ignore them the best we can in favor of our passion that lifts us up? Doing something that brings us joy is something we all want. Some of us have found that one thing, and some of us haven't. Even if we haven't found it, just the fact that we're consciously looking for our passion, allows us to access the immense energy our passion produces. Whatever stage we're at, our passion causes us to be more in the moment, which causes us to feel things more. Since we're accessing a very specific part of ourselves, our emotions are highly elevated. When everything is raw and out in the open, we're forced to deal with what does and doesn't serve us; especially if we've found our passion because it's the ultimate thing that does. Loneliness never serves us, because it makes us focus on what we don't have. At the same time, it's an emotion we must honestly admit to having, before we can recognize it and let it go. Letting go of what doesn't serve us, is how we find our passion in the first place.

We must remember letting go is a constant process, not a one and done proposition. This constant can overshadow our passion, but only if we let it. We can find our passion, and we can work our passion, but only if we allow ourselves to." ☺

FROM THE MIND OF CRITIC
DECEMBER 31st 2016

From the mind of critic: "Are we on the eve, precipice, apex or peak of a layed out plan for destruction, or is it something else? Are we on the eve, precipice, apex or peak of a layed out plan for creation and rebuilding? Or are we about to be destroyed by what we created? We can all hope and pray that 2017 is better than 2016. We can hope that people are more human to each other, and step on each other's necks a little less to get ahead. We can hope till the last breath leaves our body, but if we don't take it the next step from hope to action, we'll forever be waiting for Godot to save the day. Trump is a scary notion as he tries to radically and dangerously remake the country. He is not our biggest threat. Our biggest threat is the hate, ignorance, division, bigotry and nastiness that we allowed to fester, which made a Donald J. Trump administration possible. The great thing however, is all these issues we've continuously kicked down the road, are now slapping us in the face with their overtness. The opportunity to finally put down this ugliness is ours. We have the power to succeed. This knowledge should make us feel good, and less helpless. This is easy and not easy at the same time. This is a power struggle between the elites and the common person that has been raging for eons. We have a chance to take the upper hand in this battle, and show with courageously and exponentially high numbers that we won't sit idly by, we will rise up.

If we don't utilize this golden moment, and allow our system to be radically changed to benefit even less of us, then we deserve whatever happens. Whether we're on the eve of destruction or the eve of creation, it is our choice and always has been." ☺

www.ingramcontent.com/pod-product-compliance
Lightning Source LLC
Chambersburg PA
CBHW032037150426
43194CB00006B/308